A Daily Gift of Gratitude

A COLLECTION OF STORIES FROM GRATEFUL HEARTS AROUND THE GLOBE

Teresa Velardi

Published in the United States of America

Spirit Book Endeavors
c/o Authentic Endeavors Publishing
Clarks Summit, PA 18411

A Daily Gift of Gratitude
ISBN: 978-1-955668-49-1 (Paperback)
      978-1-955668-50-7 (eBook)

A Daily Gift of Gratitude

He is a wise man who does not grieve for the things which he has not; but rejoices for those which he has.
Epictetus

Acknowledgements

I'm grateful to every one of the contributing authors! This compilation of powerful stories and gratitude practices could not be possible without you.

Nick Koridis, your heart for the beauty of the evening sunset is all over the cover of this book. Thank you for the time you spend looking through the lens as God creates the most magnificent paintings for us to enjoy. The north shore of Long Island will always be "home," and now we get to share a glimpse of it with the world for years to come. I'm honored, and beyond grateful you said, "Yes!"

Peggy Willms, there are no words that even begin to express my gratitude. You, my friend, are a gift! I am beyond blessed to have you in my world. Thank you for everything you did to help make this book possible. It's just the beginning, my friend!

Introduction

I've learned to pay attention to the whispers. I know it's God guiding me. I'm grateful I've drawn near to him. Several years ago, He whispered about this Daily Gift Book Series. Gratitude first!

Although I was paying attention, it wasn't at the top of my list. After a while, the whisper got a little louder, and I knew I couldn't wait any longer.

I know what happens when I ignore the whispers of God. Trust me; He knows what's best. I spent many years suffering because I chose not to listen to one of His whispers. Not because God punished me but because I ignored the whisper when He said He had "something so much better for me." But I was stuck in "the what ifs" and the "BS" (Belief System) that I wasn't worthy of being blessed with the goodness of God. I've since learned. So, now, I listen to His whispers.

These stories are gathered from people worldwide.

What they have in common is Gratitude!

Grateful Hearts!

Each one is precious to me.

Enjoy them.

My prayer is that yours, too, is or will become a Grateful Heart!

The Grateful Hearts Community

What is the Grateful Hearts Community

One of the definitions in Webster's dictionary for community is:
A group linked by a common policy.

The common policy for The Grateful Hearts Community is Gratitude!

Gratitude is, according to Webster:
The state of being grateful: THANKFULNESS

Then, Webster, what is Grateful?
a: appreciative of benefits received
b: expressing gratitude

Appreciation, Gratitude, Thankfulness…. Yes, please! I'll have some of that! Why? Because grateful hearts are happier than those that aren't grateful. I like happiness, and I like abundance… yes, abundance! When we are grateful, there is always enough, even more than enough. Without gratitude, there is never enough.

It's a mindset, a perspective of how we see our lives.

Whether you already have a grateful heart or want to have one, you are in the right place when you become part of The Grateful Hearts Community.

Daily inspiration, questions, quotes, scripture, and more are just a few reasons to be part of this community.

Check out our Facebook Community http://bit.ly/Grateful-Hearts

Or visit our website: TheGratefulHeartsCommunity.com

If you believe it'll work out, you'll see opportunities.
If you don't believe it'll work out, you'll see obstacles.
Wayne Dyer

A Gratitude Transformation

by Vincent A. Lanci

*G*oing to school for finance, I was hyper-focused on how much money I could earn after commencement. A few days before what should have been my last undergraduate semester, my life changed forever.

I was the victim of a hit-and-run accident while walking home. I suffered a Traumatic Brain Injury (TBI) and a broken leg. At first, there was speculation from the doctors as to whether I would make it through the first night. Once I did, their concerns switched to whether I would ever be able to go to the bathroom on my own, walk, or talk properly again.

I went from riding an arm bicycle each morning and relearning the alphabet to returning to school just months later. I was previously a student who could look over the material a day or two before an exam and earn a satisfactory grade. I was now a student who had to read, write, and type—repeatedly—to retain a fraction of what I previously could. I had to rewire my brain. I eventually became grateful for my new process and overcame the frustration.

My view of *gratitude* changed during this transformative experience. I became more grateful for things I previously took for granted.

I became grateful for being alive.

I became grateful for being able to walk.

I became grateful for being able to talk and use the bathroom on my own.

During my second chance at life, I am grateful to be in the position to use my story and experiences to help others. Success looks different to everybody. I am grateful that I can prioritize seeing family, create mental health books for students of all ages, and I'm grateful for the opportunity to be a part of this collaboration.

Faith
OVER
Fear

Light Shines Brightest
in the Darkest Times
by Aljon Comahig

*A*t times we felt defeated even though the battle wasn't over yet. In these crucial times, miracles can happen that may change your life.

A few months before my 18th birthday, I was diagnosed with heart enlargement that I inherited from my father. It was the worst and darkest time of my life. I could barely walk, breathed heavily, and couldn't sleep without pillows piled behind my back to elevate my chest.

During those times, I had no plan, dream, or intention to fight this disease. I asked my parents if I would die, but they did not respond. Every day was the same routine; sleep, rest, watch the sunset, and wait for the moon.

One day things changed. While searching for entertainment on my computer. I stumbled upon a Japanese comics anime. I enjoyed the stories and the art. I read one episode each day!

As a person who never had a gift for doing art, I decided to learn the art from online videos. Though frustrated, I felt challenged and connected to create stories and draw. I decided I wanted to be an artist, but I had to live longer to do that.

I prayed every day. "Lord God, if you have no intention of taking my life, please help me become an artist. I want to share beautiful stories with children and make a difference in the world."

God was with me, and I improved daily. I attended college, studied animation, and graduated a few years after.

I am very grateful that God continues to shine the brightest on my purpose to make a difference in this beautiful world during the darkest times.

Sometimes, life can be difficult and unpredictable. Be grateful for challenges because you never know, they might be the turning point in your life.

A glad heart makes a happy face;
a broken heart crushes the spirit.
Proverbs 15:13-15

The Thousand-Kilowatt Smile
by Erica Lewis

A smile is infectious. In my experience, it is rare to encounter someone who embodies gratitude, graciousness, joie de vivre, and good energy with whom you can feel the power of their radiance and love.

Years ago, I attended a salsa social. There were classes in break-out rooms as well as social dancing in the main room. I joined a Salsa Shines class to learn new moves and dust off the cobwebs. When I walked in, the instructor, "FM," was already leading the group in a jam session, and I was encouraged to jump right in. I noticed the bright smile on his face and the feeling he radiated. I love dancing, and his infectious smile amplified my joy. At the end of the hour, he greeted us and emphasized that life was happening in the present moment and to take full advantage of it. I left that night with a deep impression of FM and started to follow him on social media.

Until a few nights ago, when I saw FM and his group perform on stage., I had forgotten about the social salsa experience. Not only was the performance electric, but it also reminded me of his other gift from years ago - his thousand-kilowatt smile and embodiment of gratitude.

Two years ago, he had major heart surgery. Fast-forward to the present time, he has triumphantly returned to dancing wholeheartedly with high energy. His embodied gratitude and practice of living fully in the present likely led to his miraculous recovery.

Thank you, FM, for reminding me what it feels like to radiate gratitude from within. Some people truly are lights in this world, and we never know the impact we have on others.

5

A New Day
by Sophia Long

I'm taken back to the ripe age of six years old. Naïve and unaware, yet joyful and silly, I hadn't a care in the world outside of sidewalk scrapes and the taunting of my older brother. I wanted so badly to grow up and do it all my way. Today, I often daydream about returning to that blissful and unaware time.

Much of my family passed away in my adolescence. Cancer, health conditions, and a few tragic circumstances framed my childhood. I could see no escape. I buried myself in my memories, idealizing the past. If I close my eyes, I can return to those idyllic times. When I'm missing my loved ones, I turn to those images and receive comfort, knowing it maintains their spirits in my body and soul. As I age, I recognize that some of these moments will fade, and my fear of losing what is left can overwhelm me. I hold onto the images that dance through my mind.

I've adapted as I've grown. I choose to move forward, and I cannot truly do that if I have one foot facing backwards. I understand now that the words I tell myself matter; I must remember when I start to fall into a pattern of self-deprecation or persistent anxiety. I had a *wonderful* early childhood, followed by an adolescence full of sorrow. Just for today, I will bask in the beautiful memories that remain without worrying about the future or focusing on the hurt.

As an adult, my contentment flourishes with both feet facing forward. It's okay for me to keep the memories of lost loved ones close to me so long as I don't lose myself in their remembrance.

As we express our gratitude, we must never forget that the highest appreciation is not to utter words but to live by them.
JFK

Abundant Faith and Gratitude
by Gloria Sloan

L iving a life of gratitude awakens in me a peaceful spirit. I rejoice in knowing that my past has prepared me to live with a grateful heart. I know that every day presents a new opportunity to share the gift of thankfulness. I am mindful of why gratitude is so important to practice because it helps me appreciate the abundance of blessings in my life.

One day my journey took a big step into the world of uncertainty, reminding me that throughout life, we will have shifts and changes. Life always has something to teach us. I learned to cope with new challenges in my life and used them to build hope and pillars of strength. My soul became firmly anchored in my faith through prayer and trust in God. It was faith that opened my heart to witness the power of gratitude.

I began to exercise the powerful gift of gratitude actively, intentionally, and consistently in every possible situation. Giving thanks has become an endless and perpetual feeling for me. It is more than a routine act or expression, but a divine loving emotion aligned with my spirit. Gratitude has guided me through tragedies, heartbreak, disappointments, difficulties, stress, and pain. Being thankful is the foundation that supports me during happy times, peaceful moments, and joyful celebrations. It allows me to show genuine appreciation for the gifts I receive from others.

I believe the art of gratitude, when practiced, can evolve into acts of generosity, forgiveness, and compassion. It leads to fulfillment in life. It has transformed my journey through life by bringing me a sense of wholeness.

I Left Everything to Blind Faith
by Fran Asaro

I was petrified. I left it all: my marriage of fifteen years, two lucrative businesses, security, and the familiar. For what? Why would this fearful woman, who couldn't even be left alone in her house at night, take such a chance on the unknown?

I was "guided to," that's why. I was in my mid-thirties, living a comfortable life. But somehow, I knew it wasn't truly my life. There was something more for me. I said YES to the opportunity to move on, and the ball started rolling fast. Of course, I questioned my sanity along the way. But even when I felt lost, I kept going. When would all my sacrifice pay off?

I became a life and business coach, a vocation that had been calling my name for as long as I could remember. However, it took me many years to discover a version of helping others that fit me best.

One day I got a message telling me to make videos. I immediately said, "YES!" I learned how to become a content creator. I failed often, but I loved it. I kept going for eleven years.

As a woman in her sixties, I was prompted to help other mature women leave their legacy on YouTube. Initially, it scared me. However, the "Senior Tuber Alliance" is now launched. There has been an overwhelmingly positive response to my vision to help seniors thrive.

I am grateful for the wisdom and guidance that helped light my path. I am grateful I learned to say YES while struggling with resistance, fear, and doubt. All I needed was to have blind faith.

I am also grateful to enjoy two of my loves—creating video content and helping others do the same.

Present in Universal Presence
by Eileen Bild

*L*ife has a way of knocking on our door. When we are busy doing, not being, life passes us by. If we ignore the signs, one day we will be pushed to "wake up." This awakening may turn our world upside down. I believe we go through a breakdown so that the magic of a breakthrough can take us to another level of being.

My breakdown came in my mid-thirties. I seldom refilled my personal and spiritual well. As a result, my body responded with a debilitating condition known as fibromyalgia. After a lengthy period of suffering, my will kicked in. With fists to the sky, I declared, "Take me or heal me."

It was not my time to go! I am here to inspire others to have faith in the divine plan. I went to my roots, breaking down my beliefs and conditioning to build a new foundation. Eventually, my breakthrough came. As my world shifted into a new way of life, I studied and put into practice important techniques

My daily routine includes:

- Meditation to clear my mind and focus.
- Set an intention for my day with a positive attitude.
- Start my day in nature and be present with the animals, plants, and water.
- Purposefully give gratitude for everyone and everything in my life.
- Listen to my intuitive voice and pro-actively listen "for" other people.
- Ensure my boundaries are understood by others.

- Check my confidence and put into place actions that will make it stronger.
- Leave the past in the past, step into the future with each decision/action.
- Smile and stay heart-centered throughout my day.
- End my day in nature, releasing all emotions through grounding and centering.

Live life to the fullest. It is the only one you have!
Eileen Bild

I CAN →AND→ I WILL

A Blessing in Disguise
by Sylvie Plante

I am grateful for all the moments in my life, and there were quite a lot, that seemed negative at the time and yet were instrumental in making me who I am today. They were blessings in disguise. One such moment, in the early stages of my career, was losing my job in 1983. This forced me to leave my hometown and move to Montréal six hundred miles away.

I worked for the main employer in my small Quebec North Shore hometown, and I was living a good life. At some point, the company needed to restructure to improve efficiency. At first, I was hoping to keep my job. However, with an anticipated reduction of over 10 percent of the staff and my being a relatively new hire, I realized that I might lose my job. That came about on November 4, 1983. The very next day, I took my car and went to Montréal to find a new job.

I started a job at VIA Rail on January 4, 1984. My human resources career started at the same company a few years later. At the beginning, my salary was lower, and my expenses had exploded as I had lived with my parents before moving. I moved my way up in the company and started studying in the evening at the university to acquire human resources education.

This was the start of an amazing international career in the corporate world of human resources. I have held very senior positions in which I got to travel the world and meet amazing people, many of whom became friends with whom I am still in contact to this day.

Gratitude is a powerful catalyst for happiness.
It's the spark that lights a fire of joy in your soul.
Amy Collette

Hidden Treasure

by Cyndi Wilkins

*I*n my work as a muscular therapist, I always remain grounded and focused when working deeply within the muscles and tissues, as there is the potential for releasing deep-seated memories for the client.

Occasionally, what comes to my awareness is my own buried trauma, which is why I find this work just as healing for the giver as it is for the receiver.

One morning, I was working very deeply on a client while she rested quietly. In that silence, I became aware of a past memory.

I was a letter carrier for the post office, and all city routes were being restructured. That meant all jobs had to go up for rebidding. I lost my route to someone senior to me. Unfortunately, I inherited his route in a nasty area of the city. I was crushed.

Just remembering those days made my heart sink. It was such a devastating time in my life. My job, my home, my relationship—poof! *Gone.*

Why my home and my relationship? Because I could not let go of my anger. I let it eat away at me, destroying my relationship, and eventually leading to the sale of the home we shared. That experience was a call to change. Not just in my job situation, but also a change in my *thinking.*

Fear had brought that memory to the surface, as my current partner and I were struggling with another job loss. I recognized the opportunity to release the pain and help my partner in doing the same.

That shift in perception gave me a sense of peace while being supportive in a committed relationship. That is the harmonious nature of my work. People helping people, one hidden treasure at a time.

Downsizing
by Susie Marsh

*L*ife is challenging. It's hard to face up to the fact that your home, where you brought up your lovely daughters, is too expensive to run any longer. It's an even bigger blow to be told by a barrister that you have to release some capital so that your ex-husband doesn't have to pay for maintenance anymore.

The barrister suggested I move into a small semitrailer in the middle of Leeds. I told him, "I would rather be poor and stay in my house backing onto fields with the neighbors I love."

"This is not an option," he sternly replied. "What is your smaller dream home?"

"To live in London near the daughters—nice quiet area, two beds, Juliet balcony."

"You can't afford that!" says he.

"Well to live by the sea, hear the sea, and see the sea"

"Sorry. You can't afford that either"

Funny how being told "you can't" sets up a challenge. The barrister made me realize my true dream.

I write this from my duplex apartment in a sleepy town on the South Coast of England. The sun streams in through the open balcony doors. I can see the rippling sea. I hear the gentle lap of waves as the tide creeps up the beach. Steps lead down the cliff face so that I can swim in this little piece of heaven! I am so grateful for being told "You can't afford that."

I made it happen. I moved 300 miles south to a place I had never visited before. I learned that no one can take away the happy memories of home. I always carry them with me. Now I build new times, appreciating the peace, the ever-changing view, my happy new home. God bless my barrister.

Friends are the siblings God never gave us.
Mencius

Grateful for Friends

by Melissa Zabower

*N*ine years ago, my body started to disintegrate. In the midst of great pain, I was diagnosed with a strong, aggressive form of psoriatic arthritis. Within six months, my hands became claws, my jaw fused shut with ankylosis, and fatigue clouded every day. As a middle school teacher, I had energy only for my job—and that just barely. I ate peanut butter bread for dinner. My apartment was a mess. I was overwhelmed with what my life had become.

But I was not alone. God surrounded me with a host of people. I had someone to help with meals, another friend to do the laundry, another to clean, and another friend to help with the overwhelming amount of paperwork required to apply for disability. My students carried my books for me. I could call any number of people to drive me to doctors' appointments.

My life has settled into a status quo, so to speak. It is by no means easy. But I am so thankful that God has put these people in my life. God holds me when I cry, and for everything else, He has given me friends.

Learning Through the Darkness
by Samantha Larkin

I had no idea I was entering a dark time or that it would last nearly three years. God stopped my finances and took everyone from my life aside from one person.

Why? Why would He do that? Was I so off course that my life needed a reset? I had gotten off course just a little, but enough to not be in the will of God for my life. I usually describe this time as bleeding black. The pain I had inside from my parents, family, relationships, and Christian friends had created a thick wall. God cannot use us when we have erected walls to protect our hearts from being hurt.

Jesus literally stopped my life. It was a very painful and scary time. I was not able to get any work. I was lonely and hurting. This caused me to be on my knees daily and to get back into a habit of being in his Word daily. I got closer to Jesus than I ever had been. For the first time, all the satanic voices stopped. I stopped hearing the lies: "You're not good enough." "You'll never make a living doing portraits." "You're not worthy of being loved."

Midway through this time, I heard God's voice clearly for the first time in all my journey with him since I was six years old. I learned to hear the Holy Spirit and became sensitive to His leading. In order to keep as close as I was to Him, I walked a year-long journey to forgive every one that had ever hurt me up to that point. As horrible and painful as this was, it had to happen for Him to speak through me as he does now. I am so grateful that God used that painful time so that I could reach others for Him.

23

For I consider that the sufferings of this present time are not worth comparing with the glory that is to be revealed to us.
Romans 8:18 ESV

Grateful for Eternity
by Alison Treat

L ast night I dreamt my sister called me. Or at least, her name scrolled across the screen of my phone as it rang. I answered and heard no reply. Even in my dream, I knew it couldn't be her, but I still forced the words from my throat, "Who's there?" Then I woke up.

Grief comes in waves. The waves seem to diminish with time, but sometimes a big one will come out of nowhere and take me under.

Yesterday, my cousin let me know his mother, my favorite aunt, had passed away. She was very old and had been very much not herself for the past few years. She lived a long, full, wonderful life. I had been prepared for this news to come sooner. Last November, I would have guessed that the next funeral I would attend would be my aunt's. Instead, on December 20, I found myself at my little sister's funeral, trying to hold it together and comfort my children, who had just lost *their* favorite aunt. Ten months later, my sister is on the other side, welcoming our aunt to heaven. The grief hits me fresh. I will never see her name scrolling across my phone again.

We're not meant for this world. We're not meant for this grief. Our years, be they twenty-nine or ninety-something, are just a blip when compared with eternity. I'm grateful for these loved ones and the roles they played in my life here on earth. I'm grateful to know I will be with them again someday when I finally leave this old world behind.

For Such a Time as This
by Emily Manuel

*I*n 2020 the world paused, and I watched the news in anticipation. I remembered something my mentor had said: *Focus on the solution, not the problem.*

I started reflecting on my life journey and how far I had come. I recalled standing at the pharmacy counter to pick up one of my daughter's seven medications. The clerk placed it on the counter and said, "It's $100." I did not have that money. We had recently returned from the NICU on Oahu, where my daughter had been for three months. I had no cash and no room on my credit card. I couldn't keep the tears from streaming down my face.

The pharmacy clerk said, "Let me call the hospital and see what we can do." As she walked away, I prayed, "God, if you can help me take care of my daughter, I'll find ways to give back. If I have no money, I will give my time to help others."

Because of what I had been through, I kept serving the community. God had surely delivered on his promise. So, during the pandemic, when many lost their livelihoods, I was able to serve the hurting. I found an amazing church that poured into our community, and we reached many people during their time of need. Hope Collective served hot lunches and distributed groceries through partnerships with local food banks.

God is truly an awesome God. I am so grateful for the people and the mentors he put in my life to guide me. He mapped out everything and completely orchestrated my life. He prepared me through trials and adversity. He knew long before I did that he was preparing me for such a time as this.

Gratitude makes sense of our past,
brings peace for today,
and creates a vision for tomorrow.
Melody Beattie

Finding Stability
by Marissa Lynn Bartley

*T*here I was, an innocent four-year-old on her tippy toes, arms wide open, reaching for a hug from my momma, holding back the tears that filled her eyes as she voiced the exact gentle words the little girl already expected to hear. "Everything is going to be okay," and I knew that. Still, I couldn't help but wonder how long it would take.

Stability is the glue binding every aspect of my life; financial, mental, physical, social, and educational. It affects my overall goals and ambitions so profoundly that the entirety of each aspiration and expectation I've created for myself embody the word.

My story is very different from the people I surround myself with, and I'm thankful for that. I'm proud that I can peek at my past, holding nothing but appreciation in my heart. I'm grateful for the nights I laid awake in the middle of winter, shivering as I begged God for nothing more than for my mom to return from work with enough money to pay the electric bill. I'm thankful for the scorching summer days dripping sweat the entire three miles we had to walk so we could bring groceries home. More importantly, I'm grateful for every friend and family member willing to go the extra mile to make my brothers and me feel involved, even if Mom couldn't be in the first row at the competition or cheer me on during my games.

There wasn't much stability growing up in a single-parent household. I lived through the exact opposite of what I see for my future. My constant search for stability has led me to pursue my dream of nursing while furthering my psychology education. I'm happy to be able to look back at the four-year-old me, grateful that everything IS going to be okay.

TODAY *anything is* POSSIBLE

Gratitude for Life
by Filomena Tripp

I was born in 1955. My arms and one leg did not develop. From the start, the doctors said that I would not live long. I surprised everyone by living. Then I was told there were many things I could not do, such as going to school or playing with other children. The list was long.

Children and adults ridiculed me because of the way my body looked. I had a different-looking body, but I was still a person with feelings, dreams, and goals.

Something inside told me that people had the wrong impression of my abilities. As an adult, I began to figure out my life apart from these false beliefs. I was depressed and afraid to live fully. I did not love myself. All the rejection had led to this.

One day, while at my lowest point in life, I prayed deeply. I did not want to live the way I was living. I was worthy of a happy life. It was up to me to act on my own behalf and change the way I saw myself.

I wanted to become the person I was created to be, so I did it!

Today I am grateful for all the suffering I endured. Without pain, I may not have stopped believing the lies about myself. Pain fueled my determination.

When I say that I suffered, I am telling the truth. When I say that I overcame my painful life, I did. I am proof that we have choices. For me, it began with leaning on God and learning to love myself as I am.

If I had not nurtured inner gratitude, especially for my life, my circumstances would have destroyed me. I could not let that happen.

With gratitude, we learn self-worth.

Things do not happen TO you.
They happen THROUGH you.
You are the co-creator of everything in your reality.
Gordana Biernat

The Power of Gratitude
by Gail Vilcu

*G*RATITUDE is a state of being!!!

When we fall into deep states of negativity, we must transform that energetic state in order to realign with the magical state of gratitude. This is achieved when we become aware of the negative energies that are empowering our bodies. We must allow this energetic state to move into and through our body with focused intention thru breath and visualization and realign those energies with a deeper positive state of peace and happiness. This is when we let go and reach a state of gratitude. This is significantly heightened during times of great challenges or sorrow.

When we find ourselves in challenging situations that leave us in a state of negativity and perpetual fear or frustration, we are living outside the realm of gratitude. When taking those challenges and transforming them to the exact opposite of their current state, you are immediately moving through and into a positive state of gratitude.

Everything happening to us at any given moment is a learning lesson for a particular purpose. A life lesson that guides us closer to our positive state of being.

In this state of being, we raise our vibration, and when we raise our vibration, we move into a deeper state of gratitude which puts us into the great manifestation state. It's in this very place that magic happens. And that is the incredible power of being grateful.

Have a fabulous and blessed day full of GRATITUDE.

Grateful

Grateful in Weakness
by Kristi Tornabene

I thought I was going to die a miserable death. Lou Gehrig's disease runs on the paternal side of my family. Two of my cousins died before the age of 70. Many people sail right through middle age into their nineties with no problems. I wanted to do that, too.

In addition to ALS, my family also has a history of diabetes, osteopenia, inflammation, and arthritis. My father and grandmother lived in extreme pain. My father lived in a nursing home for the last three years of his life. Diabetes runs on my mother's side of the family.

From age 55-58, I could not bend over to tie my shoes, put on my pants, or turn my head to look for oncoming traffic. I was also in perimenopause. Added to that, I was always hungry!

I decided to learn more about the symptoms and treatments to not only avoid Lou Gehrig's disease, but to improve my overall health. I needed to reduce inflammation, improve my nutrition, manage my mental health, and stress factors. I decided I would focus on all these areas. I became frustrated with diet protocols and trying every natural product. Methods the "professionals" pushed on social media or television exhausted me and didn't work. I became so frustrated with advertisements luring the public into believing that one thing was the magic cure.

The concept of eating according to your blood type made sense to me. It was more scientific than some of the other so-called cures. We all have different body types, diseases, and illnesses. Therefore, food needs are not the same for every body or every blood type. Working through a process, and keeping track, I created a system. I now use this knowledge to help others. I am grateful I have the Lou Gehrig's gene.

To the world you may be one person;
but to one person you may be the world.
Dr. Seuss

Grateful for My Mom
by Dickie-Lee Tran

I haven't been speaking much to my mom lately. I reached out to her, but she's not the same mom I used to know. It's always a quick call, ending with, "I love you, Mom. I'm here if you need me."

Recently, as I was going through my emails, I found an email from my mom. It said, "Hang in there. One day you'll look back at this situation, and you'll be in a better place." It was a reply to an email I sent her on August 2, 2013. I was in shock. I was going through a difficult divorce when I sent the original email. I told her I wanted to throw in the towel and go home to Maui. I couldn't leave at the time because I shared custody of my daughter with my ex-husband. I was living from paycheck to paycheck and having a horrible time financially. I remember sending this email to her because my eldest daughter had taken money reserved for emergencies. She was hungry and needed to buy food. It's unlike me to get angry, but I did. I took a step back and realized what I had done, and I apologized to her for getting angry. That's the day I sent this email to my mom about the difficulties I was going through.

I can now reflect on when I wrote this email to my mom; she was right. I look back at that time, and today I am a different person, a stronger person, and in a better place in my life. My mom was there for me then and still is to this day.

A Garden of Gratitude
by Colette Srebro Hughes

*I*t's the hottest dog day of the summer. Gooey sweat dribbles down my face like maple syrup on a stack of golden-brown pancakes. My yellowed t-shirt and faded blue jeans are splattered with muddy muck as I mix the perfect batch of manure tea.

Old Farmer Joe gave me this recipe years ago. Just blend a few cow flops with water. Infuse with a couple shots of Jack Daniel's. Steep well. Scoop and pour. That old-fashioned tonic is downright exhilarating! But it's not for me, it's for my vegetables and flowers. I'm a gardener.

My neighbors across the lawn think I'm crazy. But I say there's so much more to gardening than planting seeds and fertilizing. The garden patch can be a great diversion from any frustration or argument. The angrier I am, the better my garden. Like a ferocious gladiator, I stomp, claw, cut, and divide. The outcome is glorious. Not only do I witness a resurrection of seedlings, but I also experience a renewed spirit as the rhythm of life reaches from the dirt to my soul.

Acts of kindness are born from my garden to restore broken relationships. Who can stay angry after one juicy bite of a home-grown, vine-ripened tomato? Or one whiff of the heavenly scent of fresh flowers and herbs? Roses. Lilies. Sweet peas and forget-me-nots. Parsley, sage, rosemary, and thyme.

"Here is what I have seen: It is good and fitting for one to eat and drink and to enjoy the good of all his labor in which he toils under the sun" (Ecclesiastes 5:18 NKJV).

God's good earth. A gift from God who keeps me busy with the joy of my heart.

My heritage. My garden. My gratitude.

The meeting of two personalities is like the
contact of two chemical substances;
if there is any reaction, both are transformed.
Carl Jung

Healing a Broken Heart

by Shannon Barker

*O*ur marriage felt like a lifeless frozen tundra. How in the world did we even get here? These thoughts were tumbling through my brain while on an obligatory anniversary dinner. I sensed that he was experiencing similar thoughts as we politely exchanged forced small talk.

The next morning, I rolled over to face him and asked the scariest question of my life. "Do you believe this marriage worth fighting for?"

It took him an eternity to process the question. He finally responded with, "How do we do that?"

While not the reply I anticipated, it was the perfect answer. Neither of us knew how to navigate our way out of this place alone. Using that question as a springboard for many conversations that followed, we learned that the first steps for us were vulnerability and honesty. This was new and terrifying territory.

We discovered that when you feel like you are in a place of scarcity, looking for things to be grateful for can soften a hardened heart. We had both felt a lack of connection and understanding from our partner. Instead of looking for missed connections, we began to hunt for things to be grateful for. We decided to try to find ten things a day and to verbalize our gratitude for them.

This practice taught us a lot about each other. He learned that my love language is more about acts of kindness (he brings me coffee each day) and his is physical touch (hugs are now frequent and freely given). We started our daily gratitude practice a decade ago, and it has transformed our marriage. By seeking the good, we found it in our relationship and built up from there. I could not be any more grateful for that.

Becoming Heart-Centered
by Markus Wettstein, MD

*F*or me, gratitude was a learned skill in the beginning. Essentially, I was so busy in my head that I never allowed myself to be grateful for anything. I guess there was a sense of entitlement as I was working hard.

I must admit that after my 30-year marriage ended and I lost interest in my career, the voice of my heart was mute. My interests led me to research into scientific exploration of spirituality. Only then did I discover the field of mind/heart coherence.

For some, a good balance is already established. I needed scientific tools. There are apps for that. The one I chose uses a meditative approach with feedback.

Over time, I started recognizing "the voice of my heart." It is difficult to describe as it is certainly not a voice in my head. Rather, it is firstly a state of calmness. Secondly, there is a feeling of unity. The best way to describe it is the sense that nothing is random. Lastly, if I am lucky, there is an insight that is rare.

Even if there is no "Divine Inspiration," the process leaves me much less anxious, and I spend more of my life in an enjoyable and creative state.

I have received feedback from folks that known me for a while. This affects my ego very positively. In turn, the ego started allowing for a relationship between the heart and the mind to develop.

The process of heart-felt gratitude started to emerge. The beauty of it is that true gratitude is "heart infused." There are no second thoughts. It is a cozy feeling to experience this gratitude.

At this point, I am grateful for my divorce, which gave me the freedom to develop myself. The challenge now is to find gratitude in other negative events. I know I have a long way to travel.

Gratitude is the healthiest of all human emotions.
The more you express gratitude for what you have,
the more likely you will have even
more to express gratitude for.
Zig Ziglar

Losing It All—Gaining More

by Peggy Willms

*D*ivorce isn't easy for anyone. After a two-year marriage, I divorced a man I had known (or not known) for twelve years. I sought all the qualities I believed I was missing and learned they were absent for a reason.

Being a responsible, truthful, and loyal person is my framework. When I began my relationship with my ex-husband, I assumed he was made up of the same thread. As a serious, overworked woman, I knew I needed to have more fun, worry less, and enjoy the moments of life. I found a class clown to fit the bill. Unfortunately, he was also an irresponsible, deceptive liar. After the divorce, he "gifted" me with a half-a-million-dollar bankruptcy and foreclosure.

When you begin a relationship clouded in "he's everything I want," you might miss the "he is everything I need." After losing the house, the car, and—literally—the dog, I couldn't believe I was starting over at age forty-three. Yet, my faith in God pulled me through. He has taught me that there is always a reason. I came out stronger, smarter, and braver than I ever imagined. Being more aware of internal and external language is now at the forefront of my assessment of relationships, whether they are personal or professional.

Gaining confidence in my intuition has propelled me to happiness beyond compare. I no longer accept working relationships that do not serve me, and I am beyond grateful for the man God gifted to me eleven years ago. I took a risk, trusted again, and this man has never wavered from protecting my heart, supporting my passions, and building my belief in mankind. It is likely a gain when you feel God has handed you a loss.

Don't Let Go of Yourself
by Sharla Charpentier

F or most of my life, I played the role of a good daughter, family member, student, girlfriend, friend, and employee. To cope with the anxiety and pressure of these standards, I took my first drink in middle school and discovered that intoxication allowed me to let go of my inhibitions. I held it together for years, being perceived as outgoing, confident, ambitious, and successful.

In my attempt to please others, I also neglected to listen to my gut. There was pressure to attend law school, get married, and have children.

When I became divorced at thirty-eight, I fell apart. My bipolarism advanced. I lived in a state without family, had four kids relying on me, and worked endless hours. I had no clue how to take care of myself in a healthy manner, so I used alcohol "to survive."

By the grace of God, I did not kill myself or anyone else from drunk driving, did not get arrested, lose custody of my children, or lose my job. But I did lose myself: identity, spirit, and self-worth. I finally realized that something had to change – not for myself (not yet) but for my children.

For my fortieth birthday, I was given the greatest of gifts – desperation, and I surrendered. Walking through the doors of Alcoholics Anonymous was one of the first times I put myself first. I began a path of therapy and proper medication and diligently worked on the 12-step program.

Being fully present with my children is a blessing. I have good relationships with family members and co-parent with my ex-husband in a healthy manner. I have close friends that I can trust.

Each day, I wake up with gratitude and have no plans of losing myself again.

It is God who arms me with strength
and keeps my way secure.
Psalm 18:32

Sing for your Life
by Rene Kamstra

*M*y dad, who is so important to me, had a stroke and was in the ICU. At that moment, I knew I had to return to my home in South Africa.

My husband booked us tickets for the two kids and me. While I was in South Africa, one of my girlfriends informed me that my husband of 18 years had somebody else five months pregnant. Two life-changing shocks in a row.

Once I flew back home, I filed for divorce because I could not get past the deception. I became unbelievably sad and depressed so much that one morning while in the car with my children, I contemplated ending my life. My girlfriend had a feeling in that moment that she needed to be at our house immediately. She saved our lives. She told me I needed to speak to my priest. Though I am not Catholic, I did it because I knew I needed help.

He asked me what I truly loved and what wobbled out of my mouth was that I love to sing. I am a talented singer with perfect pitch and read music well. He told me to do whatever it took and focus on singing.

Two weeks later, he called me back, sharing that the choir's lead singer was in a car accident and didn't survive. He asked me if I would fill in for the morning service. By saying yes, I ultimately became the lead singer performing in 700 weddings and funerals, leading to singing in the Vatican with a group winning an Emmy Award.

While married, my singing and career took a backseat. Today I am a very successful business consultant and life coach. What sometimes looks like the devil could be the angel in disguise.

start each day with a grateful heart

Behind Everything is a Blessing

by Marina Garcia

I walked into the grocery store at six a.m. to get my lunch for work just as I did every day. On this particular morning, when the sliding glass doors opened, stress, fear, and anxiety engulfed me. The pandemic had just started, and I was unaware of the panic that had taken hold. The desperation of people overwhelmed me as I walked thru the aisles. I felt so nauseous that I wanted to vomit. When I arrived at work, everyone was sent home for two weeks. I decided not to buy into the fear, but to be careful.

I did not go out. I wore my mask. I did everything to keep myself from getting sick. I did not want to be vaccinated, so I had to stay safe. Two-and-a-half years later, I was still safe. Until one day, I felt sick. I took a Covid test. It was positive. How could this happen to me?

As I lay sweating, my body released toxins: fear, anger, doubt— all those ugly things that held me back even before the pandemic. The next day, love and compassion filled my heart, the very things that I had been blocking. Covid was a blessing in disguise. I thanked God for the new love I felt and for replacing my anger with a joyful heart.

I am not upset about getting sick. I am grateful for a new outlook. I was in a safe place with friends and family to check on me. Covid helped me create a rock-hard foundation of faith which I carry with me today. I have a strength that surprises me. Sometimes when we get what we do not want, we get what we need. So yes, testing positive was a great blessing in disguise. Behind everything is a blessing.

*A kind gesture can reach a wound that
only compassion can heal.*
Steve Maraboli

A Miracle of Kindness

by Martine' Emmons

*H*ave you ever been truly blown away by another's kindness, love, and trust? I have, and I will never forget it.

I met a woman on the beach while visiting my dad. I am an avid walker, and there is no better place in nature for my walks than by the ocean. By chance, I would meet up with her and her dog almost daily. We hardly ever arranged it. We developed a friendship in a very short period of time.

We were talking one day about what freedom looked like to each of us. I told her that if I had the financial freedom, I would focus only on my coaching business. I had two businesses at the time, one as a life coach and one as a virtual executive assistant. She asked me why I didn't just do what I loved. I said I couldn't because I had too much debt from my education.

She then asked how much I owed, and I told her. She said, "How about I give it to you?" I said, "Wait, what?!" She said I could pay her back with a low-interest loan and we talked about the details. I was literally dumbstruck. She had only known me for a couple months at that time and was willing to trust me with a rather large amount of money.

Her generosity gave me the ability to relax, build my coaching business, and experience a true miracle of kindness. I will be forever grateful.

Grateful for the Trials
by Robin Walton

G od brought me through fiery trials
Which started in my youth.
I remember the craziness I saw
As the adults drank their booze.

I remember being kids in the local bar
When the baseball games were over,
Drinking soda from shot glasses
Thinking that we were older.

I remember the summer of 1973,
burying our sister one day.
Murdered by our neighbor
In whose house we used to play.

Hoping to ease the awful pain
The sadness of the funeral,
Mom sent me to my cousins
To get me away from the strain.

While staying at my cousin's house
Which should have been fun,
My uncle got sloppy drunk
And began pointing his gun.

I am grateful God delivered us.
We could have all been dead.
I'm thankful that the bullet missed
And hit the picture instead.

Just two years later, in 1975,
Again, a tragic loss for my mother.
Whatever peace we had was gone
As we lost our two brothers.

A creative little girl I once was,
With a tender heart for the Lord.
What life remained after my siblings died
Was gone and so was joy.

Those things shaped my heart,
Gave me an unspoken resolve.
Didn't know, at the age of nine
That trauma lay deep inside.

Once alive, this girl was dead inside,
Grappling with unspoken pain.
Then, turning my womb into a tomb
I numbed the feeling that remained.

One day I meant Jesus Christ.
Didn't even know he cared.
Grateful for his mighty love
'Cause spiritually I was dead.

Grateful I am alive today.
Seriously, I should be dead.
Deaths, cancer, and many floods
Should have put me to bed.

Grateful for the fiery trials
which built my faith in Jesus.
He healed my broken heart,
For which I sing his praises.

Not All Who Wander Are Lost
by Abby Krietler Hand

Nursing found me late in the game. My last semester of college found me on a medical mission to rural Uganda, which solidified a growing desire to pursue medicine. After four intense undergraduate years, medical school felt daunting and out of reach. Plus, I would have to take organic chemistry.

Do you know that nursing school doesn't require organic chemistry? I started slogging through community college classes, working low-paying clinical jobs, and falling utterly in love with the idea of becoming a nurse. Eight years later, I wrapped up a Master's in Nursing and accepted a position in labor and delivery. On my first day on the unit, I ran into a doctor I loved from a previous job, and in her attempt to hype me up, she announced to the entire team that I was some kind of wunderkind.

I hardly lasted six months. Given my age and education, no one was willing to offer appropriate guidance or mentorship, and I floundered. Additionally, my values were severely out of alignment with the hospital. I had invested so much time, energy, and money in this journey, but I couldn't stay.

I felt like a failure. Graduate school placed hospital nursing on a pedestal, and I deeply internalized that message. That feeling persisted while I bounced around the wellness space, exploring different avenues of health and adding new skills to my resume. Six years later, I am assembling the pieces and building a uniquely wonderful picture.

I am so grateful to have chosen this difficult path. My wanderings gave me the experience and patience to create something I needed, build a life reflecting my values and desires, and begin finding who I truly am in this world. I am grateful every damn day.

Success is not final; failure is not fatal:
It is the courage to continue that counts.
Winston S. Churchill

Walk on Water
by Frank Zaccari

*N*o one can "Walk on Water" without many people showing us where the rocks are. I am no exception.

My parents were the first and the best influencers in my life. They were first-generation Americans who lived their life with integrity. They showed my brothers, sisters, and me that life will not always be easy and is certainly not fair. We will not be able to control all the obstacles that life puts in our way, but we have total control over our effort and attitude. We saw them pick up the pieces every time life knocked them down and kept moving forward. Their message that still resonated today is regardless of what happens, do the right things for the right reasons. Those words have helped me through many difficult times.

My time in the military showed me that in order to achieve "the mission," one must first have the respect and trust of those assigned to your mission. Without respect and trust, a military mission, professional career, or personal relationship will fail.

My publishers, Kathleen (Kat) Kanavos and Teresa Velardi from WeBe Books, encouraged me to write the Business Secrets series and supported me constantly. I never dreamed of having three #1 bestselling books in one year. But Kat and Teresa believed it from our first conversation.

Melissa Van Oss, my marketing and promotion partner, is the reason we created a program to show authors how to market and promote their books. Together, we marketed/promoted seven consecutive books to #1 bestseller status in twelve months.

My daughters Stephanie and Sara who were with me through the darkest period. Despite having me as a single parent, they have become caring, compassionate, and successful women. Finally, my new wife Helen who put up with me as I wrote the Business Secrets series.

Grateful for Grace

by Michelle Rene Hammer

I am grateful. So utterly grateful for grace. The grace that set me free. I am not who I once was. GOD is changing me from the inside out.

He's the spring in my step, the joy in my heart, the hope in my soul, the sparkle in my eye.

Because he lives, I live. Because he died, I am forgiven. Before Christ, I was altogether different—influenced by others, weighed down by the pressure to do right.

Some call it *religious guilt* or *faulty theology*. I call it *prison*. A prison made of false beliefs. That was before grace set me free.

Blessed relief. Sweet assurance of a better today. A better tomorrow. A better forever.

My eyes were opened. Jesus offered me his life in exchange for mine, and I said a resounding YES.

Now! I walk with the certainty that he is for me, he does it all through me, and he is always with me.

I walk free. And help others walk free too! Life isn't perfect. Suffering doesn't end in this world. Jesus said, "In this world, you will have trouble, but take heart, I have overcome the world." (John 16:33 NIV)

I no longer go it alone. Jesus is with me every step of the way. His spirit guiding and helping, healing and forgiving. I am thankful for life in Christ now and forever. Jesus said, "I am the way, the truth and the life. No one comes to the Father except through me." (John 14:6 NIV)

When you really dig into this, everything changes. "When Jesus sets you free, you are truly set free indeed." (John 8:36 paraphrase)

Thank you, GOD, for changing everything, for changing me, and for giving me the privilege to help set others free.

Yet I am always with you;
you hold me by my right hand.
Psalm 73:23

A Delighted Heart
by Sandra Heidt

Yeah, we're dancing to the rhythm of your heartbeat
Carrie Underwood

S unday 5:00 AM, the phone rings. "Mr. Heidt, as chief heart surgeon at Tampa, General, informing you that your wife, Sandy, died twenty minutes ago."

I think of Reverend Ford's sermon from my favorite movie, *Pollyanna*, "Death comes unexpectedly."

Pollyanna changes the Reverend's demeanor, pointing out that there are 800 glad texts in the Bible. To me, a glad heart is a heart "delighted" to receive God's love. If we delight ourselves in God, He will give us the desires of our hearts. One of those desires is life. The Reverend in Pollyanna was correct, we don't know when death will come, and many times it is too late to have 'delighted' your heart in God.

I only remember the events of that Sunday as told to me. The fact is, I did die unexpectedly that Sunday morning.

At 5:10 AM, the surgeon continued the phone conversation. "I did something we practice in Med school that I never thought I would do for real. Because her surgery was the week before, her chest was easy to open; I reached in, put her heart in my hand, and massaged it with the other. Suddenly, I felt her heart starting to beat. I could feel God's hands on my hands bringing her back to life – it was a miracle".

Months later, I fully recovered; I was ready to go *dancing* to the rhythm of my heartbeat.

I am thankful to my surgeon and all those who stood by my side through this ordeal. Long ago, I chose life through Christ (John 3:16).

At an unexpected time, God granted me the desires of my heart and *life*. For that, I am eternally thankful and glad.

Gratitude for Nature
by Janine Ouellette Sullivan

*N*ature is my haven. In good times and in difficult times, being outdoors nourishes me. I am grateful to be able to experience an array of weather conditions and all four seasons. This both soothes and alerts me.

During certain natural conditions, I can sit and soak up what is all around me. Other times, I am called to act, move, and prepare. Nature is my teacher. I am grateful to have such an ancient, masterful, and generous instructor.

The sun feeds me precious vitamin D. Rain grows all that is needed. Wind and wildlife spread seed all about. I am grateful to be able to watch this gift in real-time.

Outdoors I can hear a symphony as birds sing, the wind rushes through leaves, and creatures sound their various signals.

The experiences of walking in sand, climbing a hill, swimming in a cold mountain lake, and sitting by a crackling fire in stillness feed the soul and exercise the mind.

Nature teaches gratitude as we are completely reliant on it. A deep and mutually sustaining relationship can occur between myself and nature. We depend on one another's *proper caretaking*.

I am grateful to have this awareness and desire and the ability to sustain both. "Being" in nature, with gratitude, has made all the difference in my life.

Don't you know that you yourselves are God's temple
and that God's Spirit dwells in your midst?
1 Corinthians 3:16

Now I Lay Me Down to Soar
by Debra Costanzo

*T*he airbag hit my face. My head smashed against the driver's side door of my little red Chevy Spark, and my eyes burned from the smokey after-effects of the airbag.

What had just happened? An SUV had appeared out of nowhere, delivering a direct hit to the driver's side door. Bullseye! I pushed my door open. My legs buckled. I screamed in pain. A kind man grabbed my body and said, "Sweetie, you're not going anywhere. Sit back down on your seat until the ambulance gets here. You're going to be OK."

The next thing I knew, an EMT was cutting off my skinny jeans, ankle to thigh, from my right leg.

My prayers were no different on the morning of March 13, 2020, but my day ahead was *vastly* different as were the next ten months. I sustained a brain bleed from the impact of the airbag and a right tibial bicondylar plateau fracture, which in plain language, translates to my right tibia being completely shattered.

God brought everything to a screeching halt. Everything.

After two surgeries, ten months of rehabilitation, and losing my car, job, condominium, and dreams, I moved closer to my family in North Carolina.

Each morning as I lock my condo door behind me, I humbly thank the Lord for my home, my job, and my life. I always ask Him to get me to and from work safely.

I could have lost my life. But I didn't. I could have lost my right leg. But I didn't. Graciously, the Lord gave me a new life. New dreams. He gave me the freedom to do all those things I never had time to do, such as writing this expression of gratitude.

67

BE EVER
THANKFUL

Cancer is Never Invited
by Diane M. Simard

*B*reast cancer. A stealthy, inconvenient bully that incites terror and bewilderment. A havoc-wreaker on women (and some men) of all ages.

My time in the breast cancer ring occurred in 2015 when I was 49. I was an anomaly—an enigma who didn't fit the statistical parameters since my non-aggressive grade of breast cancer was behaving aggressively. I was diagnosed as a late Stage III because my three breast tumors were two centimeters or less, yet cancer had spread to at least one axillary lymph node, perhaps as many as five. Since the tumors had a high probability of spreading throughout the rest of my body, I was prescribed the nuclear bomb treatment, a plan that was vetted and confirmed by a second-opinion medical team. Like so many other cancer patients, there was no history of breast cancer in my family.

The day I was diagnosed, I went through the typical stages of shock, denial, and anger. But I quickly realized I wanted to experience cancer deeply, capturing the reactions from strangers in the grocery store who saw me in a bandana and describing to them the nauseating smells of red onions and jet fuel that nearly made me faint in the first few days after each of my 16 chemo infusions.

Details of the excruciating sorrow I experienced every time I met or witnessed a terminal cancer patient were captured in my journal, later self-published as *The Unlikely Gift of Breast Cancer*, named one of the best breast cancer books of all time by BookAuthority.org. The experience transformed me into a clearer-thinking, purposeful business leader and forced me to ponder my mortality.

Cancer is never invited, and cancer never leaves. But I now live with intention, embracing the second chance I was given to do a more impactful job of living.

Gratitude for the present moment and the fullness of life now is the true prosperity.
Eckhart Tolle

Don't Worry, Be Happy
by Angi Currier

L ately, everything I see on television and social media, or hear in the background noise of my life, seems to send the same message. We are only here on earth for ourselves. We shouldn't be bothered, offended, or upset if someone judges us or portrays us in a certain way. Is it in our nature to receive our self-image from others?

I was bullied in my younger years for many reasons. I was short and stocky. my mom cut my hair. I had braces. I wore my older sister's hand-me-down clothes. I was a loner, and my personality was unusual. I just didn't fit it in. It didn't help that my father consistently compared me to my sister. No matter how hard I tried to deflect these feelings, it was hard. It still is at times.

As I entered adulthood, I've found that people can still be cruel. I continue to try not to let it affect me.

Humans are uniquely formed, and our personalities are predetermined by our genes before birth. So why can't people be nicer to one another? Why can't we embrace our differences?

One day, the memories of things that upset or bothered me will face. So why let it take away my happiness now?

As I think about the rest of my life, oddly, I feel grateful for some of the cruelty I sustained when I was younger. I am stronger for it. I will continue to love myself and my family. I will continue to do things that make me happy. I am thankful for those who love me unconditionally for all my flaws and quirkiness, and I pray for those who don't.

I Walked the Bridge of Tears
by Maria Wynnyckyj

Past tense of feeling lost and never to be found.
I walked the bridge of tears, only to become.

Stronger in my outlook on life and how I will take it day by day.
Coming across the other side and now looking back isn't so bad,
I will say.

Walk with me, and you shall see.
Gratitude will be what sets you free.
Because you gave yourself a chance to just be.

The pessimist sees difficulty in every opportunity.
The optimist sees opportunity in every difficulty.
Winston Churchill

Why *Not* Me?
by Leann Rhodes

*I*n 2018, I finally gave birth to my rainbow baby boy. He brought so much joy to my life. Two weeks after he was born, devastation hit. Our precious baby was diagnosed with stage four neuroblastoma, a rare childhood cancer. Time stood still as they told me they needed to immediately hook my infant to chemotherapy and insert a port into his chest. Their timeline was one to one and a half years of chemotherapy. My mind started racing, thinking of all our firsts that would be spent in the hospital instead of in our home.

Tears flowed, and anger took over. I wondered, *Why me?* After talking to a friend, she allowed me to be human but then gave me a pep talk that changed my outlook on the situation. She said, "It's not 'why you' but 'why not you'! God has chosen you to be this baby boy's mom. He chose his parents and family because He knew He could work through this situation miraculously. God will use this for a testimony."

My walk with God grew closer than it ever had been before. I started attending church during treatment and listened to what God wanted me to see and hear in this chapter. God placed the most amazing people in my life to introduce me to holistic healing and opened my mind to be willing to try something new. Our baby went for his first scans and blew the doctors away. Less than three months into treatment, his body was restored. His cancer was gone, and we could ring his end-of-treatment bell. We spent every holiday at home making memories and using his testimony to help others!

As I Am
by Marian and Jonathan Whitlock

I am mad.
I am sad.
I am confused.
I am tired.
I am happy.
I am playful.
I need a nap now.
I want to be alone.
I want to be with my friends.
I want to cry.
I am ashamed.
I have to man up.
I want to be with my family
I am excited.
This is me.
This is PTSD.
This is me getting help.
This is me helping others.
This is me being a man.
This is me thriving.
This is me understanding.
This is me loving.
This is me caring.
This is me living.
This is me coping with PTSD.

I am grateful.

Experience is a hard teacher because
she gives the test first, the lesson afterwards.
Vernon Sanders Law

Helping Out
by Anne Worth

*H*e was old and scruffy. I was surprised when he called out to me, "Ma'am, could I help you with your groceries?" My first inclination was to say, "No, thank you," thinking it might not be the best idea to let this man go with me to my car.

I had to make a split-second decision. I had not one, but two large bottles of water plus other groceries. The thought crossed my mind that even at eighty, if I needed to do it, I could defend myself against this old man.

So, I said, "Yes, thank you!"

I had a couple of extra dollars and thought I would "help him out." He unloaded my groceries, and I extended the money to him.

"Oh no, ma'am," he said. "I didn't do this for the money. I was feeling really low today, feeling worthless. You gave me an opportunity to help you. I'm so grateful. I feel like I have something to give."

Gifts in Disguise
by Jacki Long

I never thought I would say that I'm grateful for alcoholism.

How could I appreciate watching my husband self-destruct? It felt chaotic and devastating for our family and to all those who loved him. I was miserable, feeling I had to keep it all together. I was the organizer of all things: house manager, planner, shopper, and chef. I juggled full-time employment and our active two-year-old son. It was hard, exhausting work. Adding insult to injury, I discovered that my supposedly sober husband had fallen off the wagon. I knew I couldn't live this way any longer. I knew I wanted better for my son, the little one in my womb, and me.

Five years into my marriage, I finally hit rock bottom and asked my husband to leave.

Separated, pregnant, depressed, and petrified, I walked into my first twelve-step meeting. Members welcomed me with open arms. Those rooms taught me a step-by-step method to work on myself and accept my contributions. I learned to change my behavior because that was the key to my happiness.

I learned to grow from the depths of this debilitating family disease into a better version of myself. I met some of my closest friends. I have a tribe of people like me, walking a similar path. We are fiercely protective of each other.

Most importantly, I found faith in a higher power and knew I would never be alone again.

My husband walked his own journey; he never had another drink after I asked him to leave. He worked hard on himself, and we found common ground to rebuild our family together.

Ironically, over time, my darkest days turned into the most beautiful gifts of my lifetime. So, yes, I am grateful for the disease of alcoholism.

Family is not an important thing. It's everything.
Michael J. Fox

Gratitude Cultivates Blessings
by Johnny Tan

*M*y mom always taught me to be thankful for the things I received from others. What began as a gracious attitude of politeness as a child soon morphed into a natural habit of being grateful for the many happenings in my adult life.

Adopted at birth by my Malaysian mom, my life journey took me halfway around the world to attend college in the U.S. four months after my eighteenth birthday. I didn't know my gratitude odyssey was about to kick into overdrive! My life's trajectory took a sharp turn a year later with my dad's sudden passing. Circumstances our small family encountered led me to make decisions that resulted in my not setting foot in Malaysia for fifteen years.

Over those years, I met eight incredible women who became my surrogate mothers. They were my teachers, coaches, and counselors. My nine moms were the push when I was at a standstill, the guides when I was rolling, and the cheerleaders when I was inches away from various finish lines. During this time, I learned about the power of relationships, the nature of love, and the meaning of life.

How can one be grateful when life throws us a curve ball? That is simple - It is an experiential lesson to help us elevate our consciousness to the next level as we journey one step closer to our divine destiny of excellence!

Every night before I go to sleep, I review and celebrate the various blessings I experienced during the day—from getting the last container of the Deli Pizza Sauce at the grocery store to the enlightening Zoom Meeting that sets the foundation for future successful collaboration. With a smile, I doze off, knowing tomorrow will be another day to express my gratitude for more blessings!

The Brightest Light

by Andee Scarantino

*I*n the mornings of the first year of COVID-19, I would meditate in East River Park.

It was a confusing time for so many of us. Manhattan is desolate; rats that once had so much discarded food to eat now lie dead in the streets from hunger. The city, scared, mourned the losses of loved ones, whose bodies were undeservingly placed in freezer trucks stationed outside of hospitals at capacity.

I lived alone during that time. I had a job where I was caught in a proverbial rat race for over a decade. Then, the virus that would eventually kill over six million people screeched it to a halt.

It was a time of great pain and sadness, yet there was one shining light of a human who showed me how to let go, be, and cultivate peace during the storm. His name is Andy.

I'd been following Andy for a few years, and when the pandemic hit, I watched as he nobly took his place in service. Every day, he opened his life and his heart to the world. He'd do live videos of his morning movement and afternoon videos of bodyweight workouts. He read from books with passages about compassion, love, and grief. He began a meditation circle on Facebook and, without fail, showed up and led us every day.

Sangha, Andy said, meant community. That was his superpower. He crafted a beautiful container of serenity.

As I'd listen to the East River crash against the rocks juxtaposed with the softness of Andy's voice, I knew in my heart that for the first time, maybe in my whole life, that I was OK.

In a time of pain and worry, I was warmed by the light of Andy's beautiful soul.

I can't adequately express my gratitude for all he has given me.

Fear not, for I am with you; be not dismayed
for I am your God; I will strengthen you,
I will help you,
I will uphold you with my righteous right hand.
Isaiah 41:10

Practice Gratitude
by Dalia Ramahi

*P*racticing daily and momentary gratitude is the most magical form of living. This gratitude practice has saved me from devasting heartache and allowed me to process trauma and physical and emotional pain. I know that everything happens for a reason, but sometimes it's hard to process, let alone understand.

I woke up one day earlier this year unable to feel or move my legs. It happened shortly after the new year. This was after I declared I would have the most incredible 2022 ever! It was scary not knowing what was going on with my body. The worst part of it was the pain. It was pure agony. I couldn't sit up or stand and could barely drag myself with my arms because the pain was so intense. I wondered why this was happening now. I already had my gratitude practice firmly in place when this occurred, and I'm grateful I could hold onto that during the worst of it.

I learned to look beyond the pain and see what it felt like to be healed. I started being grateful for what the pain taught me about myself and my relationship with everything and everyone around me. I saw the gaps in who I was and whom I desired to be and learned from them. I grew as a person, and the more I found joy in it, the easier things became. As I learned to make peace with the pain, I started improving. This is truly the power of belief and gratitude. I gave myself permission to feel everything I needed, whether positive or negative. This is shaping up to be the most incredible year for me! Thank you, God.

wake Up AND BE awesome

Grateful for the Big Move
by Dianne Stephens

*U*pon completing my professional training as a respiratory therapist in Halifax, Nova Scotia, I was supposed to have a position waiting for me in the children's hospital there. Shortly before graduation, I was informed that the hospital had instituted a hiring freeze. My sure, secure job was no longer available. Now what? I was a big girl who was supposed to be able to look after herself now. Halifax was my home, where all my family and friends were located. The thought of having to move away was less than ideal!

In the following weeks, I began investigating hospital positions elsewhere in Canada. Multiple positions were available, but I would face a move away from home and start my professional life in a strange place. I would be completely removed from my comfort zone.

In 1990, we had only in-person or telephone interviews. After a few of these, I finally decided, and an offer confirmed it. St. John's, Newfoundland, was going to become my new home.

My clothes and a few worldly possessions were put into a moving truck, and off it went. I drove to my new city, found an apartment, and started the next chapter as a single young woman in an unknown place.

Looking back on this experience, even though it was difficult to move to a strange place, I see the huge benefit it provided. My life took a quantum leap forward the day I had to rectify my situation. Moving to that new city led to wonderful professional and additional opportunities that I could never have imagined for myself, and it all started the day I said yes!

God or the Universe never hurries and his plans,
unknown to us, are never rushed.
Carol Crandel

The Power of Rest
by Gina Lobito

*R*ecently I was reflecting on my youth. My twin brother and I were eleven weeks premature. Naturally, we needed a bit more care and tending to as infants. I had Hyaline Membrane Disease, also known as Respiratory Distress Syndrome. My parents were extra mindful when it came to my care, especially since my heart stopped beating on three different occasions, and I stopped breathing—twice while still in the NICU and once after I came home.

Over several months, my lungs grew stronger, and I could breathe independently, but the mindfulness for my health was very present. When I developed colds, the flu, and fevers in my childhood, my father always kept me home from school to rest whenever I was sick. He made me soup, or my mom made Jell-O and let me sip it when it was still warm. That was something to look forward to when I was under the weather.

My parents' care showed me the importance of self-care and rest. To this day, taking naps and resting comes very easily for me. Rest is part of my daily routine. I never really considered it self-care. However, looking back on my childhood, my father taught me self-care and the importance of resting. He simply allowed me to be ill while caring for and nurturing me when I could not do it for myself.

I am grateful that this self-care practice has become part of my day-to-day culture. I honor my body to support my wellness. I do not doubt that my culture of rest and leisure contributes to my health and well-being today.

I am grateful to my parents, who instilled the Power of Rest in me.

TOGETHER
—IS MY—
FAVORITE
PLACE TO BE

Gratitude for Living a Phenomenal Life
by Debara Bruhn Towt

*A*t a young age, a magical, loving guidance comforted me. It brought me laughter and, to this day, is my best friend…all from within me. At age six, walking home from school in a new town, I lost my way on the first day of the first grade. My mother and father had spent many days preparing me to walk home alone, but when the hour came to go home from school, I had found a new friend with the same first name. We laughed and skipped all the way to her house. As I turned to leave, I remembered my parents telling me how to find my way home. "Look for the green house on the mountain."

Alone in a cemetery, feeling hopeless, I gazed upon the statue of Mother Mary just in front of me. Kneeling, I began to pray that I might see the green house on the hill and find my way home. In prayer, I experienced a soft, comforting glow around me. It was the loving presence of a kind woman, and the words began forming inside me, encouraging me. She said, "Stand up and look up toward the mountain and you will see the green house on the hill and find your way home." I looked up, and there it was!

I've known loss and grief, having lived through many deaths. One of my daughters lived in a coma until ten years of age. Another left us at sweet sixteen in a roll-over accident. My brother had HIV in the early 1990s, and my father passed from Leukemia. This presence brought me comfort during all these difficult times. I am grateful to be alive, married to one who loves me, working every day in the ministry, and living a phenomenal life.

And whatsoever ye do in word or deed,
do all in the name of the Lord Jesus,
giving thanks to Go and the Father by him.
Colossians 3:17, KJV

I AM
By Mark Heidt

Tell me…. who are you?
Because I really want to know
Pete Townshend (The WHO)

*U*sually, we show gratitude for receiving things from others or obtaining results beyond our control. Why, then, would we be giving thanks to God for the results we, ourselves, achieved? From our "me" perspective, we wouldn't. I did it; I earned it; I am entitled to it, so I deserve all the thanks, praise, and awards.

The answer is found in Colossians 3:1-14. Therein, we discover who we are, which is indeed something we really want to know.

We are a new creation in Christ commissioned to do good works and act toward others with love and goodwill, concluding with Colossians 3:15, "Be ye thankful."

Gratitude is, therefore, more than an act of giving thanks; it is WHO we are; it is our essence, identity, our I AM.

Thankful denotes being given "favor," meaning empowered for effective success action. The power is not your own doing, not something you have earned. It is a gift made available to you by God's Grace (John 3:16).

This is a duality the world does not understand. Yes, you are to perform good work, and your effort is required. But the power to perform is not from your former self-reliant, worldly self but from the power of Christ within you.

In this way, we are both blessed and are a blessing to others.

Begin your Thanksgiving prayer not with your needs list but rather, "Here I am, Lord, send me," I am thankful.

You are powerful; you are loved. Now Be Ye Thankful.

Reframing Gratitude
by Rachelle Sweet

*T*ime is a crazy concept. Each day I watch it tick away. My life seems fleeting. How we view time can be seen through the lens of our attitude. Attitudes color the memories. Some look back only with regret.

Can we change the way we look at life? Can we reframe these thoughts and memories? The simple answer is yes! We can start with gratitude. Starting with positive memories, we can think back to a happy moment and revel in how grateful we are for that experience. We can appreciate the moment that was given to us and how it has impacted and positively shaped us. Once we have the art of reveling in the positive, we can move on to the things we view as negative. We can ask ourselves, "What was the silver lining? How did this change my life or positively impact me?" Now we can begin the process of reframing.

Thinking back to a particularly bad financial time in my life when debt collectors were calling, it felt like the end of the world. I carried that shame, guilt, and pain for many years to the detriment of my health. Negative emotions can be forever imprinted on us in gray hair, wrinkles, and chronic disease. By practicing reframing, we can begin to relieve our bodies of carrying that negativity. With that financial disaster came fiscal confidence, due diligence, and choosing business partners more carefully. I am grateful for the opportunity to become stronger and more capable. The memory of this time has shifted. I view it as a positive lesson that has shaped my life. Grateful for the opportunities and the lessons, I dust myself off, get back up, and look at my past differently.

It is health that is real wealth and
not piece of gold and silver.
Gandhi

The Story of a Girl and Her Dress
by Laura Frontiero

*F*ourteen years ago, I found a lovely Nicole Miller dress in a resale boutique. I had a formal event to attend but couldn't afford to buy a new dress at the time.

During the recession of 2007, my husband was out of work. We were stuck with a property we couldn't sell and had no money in the bank. We were just making it paycheck to paycheck, so I couldn't justify spending money on myself.

My mom gave me $200 and said, "Laura, go find yourself a dress." She knew the power of getting dressed up. She knew it would lift my spirits and boost my confidence if I could feel lovely for a night.

The minute I saw it—embroidered silk, boning in the corset top, tied with a sweet ribbon at the back—I knew this was my dress.

That special dress has been in my closet for the last fourteen years since I wore it, until last year.

My daughter wore the magic dress to her homecoming. We had it tailored to fit her. I'll never forget the little sound of delight that came from her throat the first time she tried it on. Even the tailor couldn't hide her excitement as Bella walked out of the dressing room for the first time.

She had the best night of her life.

There is power and magic to this dress. These small moments of life bring me to tears in gratitude for my family and for all the good that is still available to us, even as the world seems to be falling apart. I'm grateful the night was everything I could have wanted for my daughter. Even in times of chaos, we can find joy.

Beauty in the Storm
by Martine' Emmons

*A*fter the divorce from my children's father, I had all three children with me. For three years I was a single mom in California, and then I met my current husband. We married and moved to Michigan.

After three years, my youngest, my son, wanted to see what it was like to live with his dad and his girlfriend. The kids had been out to visit with their dad, and he wanted to stay. I was so sad, but I knew he needed the experience. I decided to fly out there and have a lengthy conversation with my ex-husband. We came to an agreement.

While we were in California, the kids and I stayed at a hotel together and we spent time with my sister. She had just become a chef. She had overcome so many challenges in her life, and it was wonderful to see her happy, and "in her glory." When she wore her chef uniform, she beamed with pride. She had found her purpose. She made us a meal and a fun, decadent dessert. The kids loved it, and so did I.

Little did we know that would be the last time we saw her. I got the call that she passed away while my husband and girls were on a little get-a-way. We had literally just toured a home (a possible vacation home) and had talked about how much my sister would have loved it. Then we get the call. I couldn't believe it. She had overcome the odds in many situations, and then she was gone.

If my son hadn't wanted to experience living with his dad, I never would have had that special time with her. This is the beauty in the storm. This is gratitude with deep hurt at the same time.

Come to me, all you who are weary and burdened,
and I will give you rest.
Matthew 11:28

Grateful for God's Provision
by Donna Guary

And my God will meet all your needs according to
the riches of his glory in Christ Jesus.
Phil. 4:19 NIV

*R*ecently I had the privilege of encountering God on a whole new level. Some wonder why I call it a privilege. It would take me on a journey of watching God provide for me daily. Life seemed to be unraveling. I was struggling financially, and I saw no way out. I fought the urge to panic. I needed to trust God and worrying was not an option. Then God opened a door for me to make additional income and assumed the money would be abundant. As it turned out, God only provided enough to care for my daily needs.

As I embraced my situation, biblical examples of God's daily provision often came to mind, reminding me that God loves us and will take care of us. "Give us today our daily bread" became my prayer. (Matt. 6:11 NIV)

If you're in the middle of a storm and can't see your way out, let me encourage you to fix your eyes on a faithful God who loves you dearly. He declares to you today that He will supply all of your needs according to His riches in glory in Christ Jesus (Phil. 4:19).

Trust Him. He is fully aware of everything you need, and His provision is sufficient for you today. He is Jehovah-Jireh, our provider!

life is
TOUGH
but so
ARE YOU

From Death to Life
by Alysia Lyons

"*I* want a divorce."

Those four words were the most devastating thing my husband could have said to me. Our son was six months old, and the words came out of the blue. Sure, we'd been fighting more lately, but how could he jump straight to *divorce*?

Something snapped inside me. Divorce seemed worse than death. I didn't bring our little boy into this world so that I could be a single mom. I didn't want him to grow up only seeing his dad on weekends the way I had.

I called my friend for help, crying hysterically. I wanted to die, but my uncle had killed himself when I was a baby. I knew I couldn't do that to my family.

My husband and I officially split eight months later, when we could no longer pretend we still loved one another.

I lost everything I had been proud of. I was a military wife and a mom. I was a leader in the top 2% of the company I worked for, and I drove a company car. Suddenly, I was getting divorced for the second time. I had lost my position and my car, and I felt like a terrible mom.

Everything I lost had been built on a foundation of quicksand, and it disappeared as quickly as I'd built it. But as these things were stripped away, I was able to rebuild my life on a foundation of deeply rooted self-love, which was something I never could have achieved inside that marriage.

Today, I am a proud mother of that amazing boy. I am happily unmarried to a man who keeps me grounded, and I am living my dream of being an author and coach.

I awoke this morning with devout thanksgiving for
my friends, the old and the new.
Ralph Waldo Emerson

One with All
Rev. P. A. Serena Hemmer, MSW, LCSW

I sat still, listening to my inner voice tell me what to write. Out of the many things I feel blessed and grateful for, the spontaneous spiritual awakening I experienced in 1991 moved to the forefront.

I went to our neighborhood Catholic church for Palm Sunday mass. I was at a turning point in my life, ending a marriage of twenty years. I was in severe emotional pain, which manifested as physical pain. At thirty-eight, I could not lift my left arm above shoulder level, and I was walking with a cane because of the pain.

Every year during Palm Sunday mass, the liturgy is the same. It tells the story of Jesus, from his triumphant ride into Jerusalem until his death on the cross. In the scripture, before Jesus dies, he calls out, "Father, forgive them for they know not what they do."

When I heard these words, something out of the ordinary happened! My spiritual heart exploded open! Comforting bright light entered my physical body. In a nano-second, I saw everything that ever was and everything that ever will be.

Then—snap—I was in the present moment, sitting on the pew, crying, as a deep sense of connectedness to everyone and everything that ever was and will be, rippled through me.

This was the beginning of my conscious spiritual journey. I was called to open to the healing Spirit of love to heal myself. Later I allowed that love to flow through me to help others as an ordained metaphysical minister, energy and sound practitioner, and psychotherapist.

I was awakened to my authentic self as infinite and unbounded spiritual energy or consciousness, one with everything. I know we are completely connected and in oneness with all that is. And all that is, is love. I am grateful.

Happiness IS Homemade

A Dream Come True
by Gerlinde Watson

I grew up in the suburbs of Melbourne, Australia. The outer suburbs—or so I thought. I discovered a few years back that it was only 15 kilometers from the CBD (Central Business District). It's funny how my sense of space and distance has never improved. As a kid, I didn't dream of living in the country. I dreamed of having a horse.

At fifteen, after selling toys in a department store at Christmas and cleaning houses for extra cash, I had saved up enough money and was ready to buy my first horse! I think back to my dad (who had no idea) and myself (who had a slim idea) sitting in the car circling ads in the weekend paper and driving around to try potential steeds. One of the few we tried that day was Karmoon, a palomino treasure listed as "not a suitable first horse." After the two of us inspected him and I rode him, we left to check the next possibility. Later, while eating pie at the closest bakery, we agreed that Karmoon it was—and bought him! My teenage heart was completely besotted. How we managed to find a treasure that I spent years with and had lots of fun with was more good luck than good management.

I am so grateful that a girl born in the city had parents like mine. They had no experience with or interest in horses. Yet they supported a strong-willed teenager's passion for making a dream come true. Many years later, horses are still in my life and fill my soul.

To make a difference in someone's life, you
don't have to be brilliant, rich, beautiful
or perfect. You just have to care.
Mandy Hale

We Will Always Be Friends
by Lori Walker

I met him nineteen years ago, after my divorce. In my eyes, he was one of those men who could never be tamed. After some contemplative thought, I decided to just enjoy the time we spent together. Live in the moment and expect nothing in return. We were free to be ourselves, with no demands or expectations.

Our motto evolved into "No matter what happens, we will always be friends." I stuck to the plan and didn't get too attached. Our lives took different paths, and we simply fell out of touch.

Five years ago, I received a text from him. He was having issues with his son and needed some advice. He wanted to see me.

It had been ten years since our last rendezvous. I had gained a significant amount of weight during that time, and I was self-conscious about my appearance. I declined his invitation. He wouldn't give up that easily. My heart melted when he said, "I don't care how much you weigh; I just want to talk to you again."

I had recently become an empty nester and was spiraling into an abyss of loneliness. I agreed to see him. I believed that I was setting myself up for heartbreak, but I pushed through the fear and did it anyway. It was the best decision I ever made. We are now closer than ever.

Our relationship will never be traditional. We will never get married. However, I can say, from the bottom of my heart, that I would rather have a friend like him than a wedding ring. My friend became my hero.

A Lesson in Joyful Living
by Kimberly Rinaldi

*I*t doesn't matter whether the glass is half-full or half-empty; a joy-filled life is about learning to be grateful for the glass! *Gratitude is a lesson in joyful living with a side of miraculous healing.*

It will take some work, and like any other practice, you'll have to practice. Will there be times you'll want to flail your arms and stomp your feet because life is unfair, and you deserve better?

You bet, but it's never been known to change the circumstances. So, practice being grateful for the glass instead.

I'm sure you don't particularly enjoy reliving experiences repeatedly while continuing to feel the anger, sadness, pain, shame, guilt, grief, fear, frustration, jealousy, envy, anxiety, regret, or feelings of low self-worth that came with them.

Did you know that you're victimizing yourself further? Every moment you carry those negative emotions, feelings, thoughts, or intentions beyond the event or when you're done with them is victimization.

It's not your fault. You didn't know – *until now.*

Your Practice

Begin with the understanding that every experience is neutral until you place a value on it. Good, bad, or indifferent, you choose. And that choice is primarily instantaneous, mostly unconscious.

The glass is how you carry the experience forward with you. You are the container for the experience. You, and only you, can powerfully and consciously choose what you carry forward, regardless of what that glass has been filled with or how it has been filled.

You see, when you own it, you can change it. The practice of being grateful for the glass gives you the miraculous ability to heal your past. No. Matter. What.

Healing your past gives you the freedom to live the life you want no matter what. It won't always be easy, but it will always be worth it. I promise.

113

Enjoy the little things
for one day you may look back
and realize they were the big things.
Robert Brault

I'm Glad I Was There That Day
by Angi Currier

One Sunday morning, I went to work early to get things ready for the day when Kyle, one of my employees, happened to come in behind me. His arms were covered in blood, and tears streamed down his face. He smelled of alcohol. He asked if he could talk to me. While talking, I discovered that he was afraid to tell his parents he was gay for fear of their rejection. He had been drinking and cutting himself with a razor to hide the pain of an aching heart. I advised him to tell his parents and get help to get him through his pain and addiction. I offered to talk to his parents with him for support, but he declined. I gave him my phone number and told him I was there for him if he needed anything else.

Later that evening, I received a phone call from Kyle letting me know that he talked to his parents and that they ended up taking him to a rehab facility for addiction two and a half hours away. He thanked me for being there for him.

A few days later, I received a visit from his parents. They thanked me for convincing their son to go to treatment and told me I had saved Kyle's life. We were all overcome with emotion.

I am so grateful that Kyle came to me for help. He moved away after treatment and is doing well. I see his parents around town occasionally and always ask about him.

Sometimes you may not know what someone is going through. I am thankful I was there for Kyle that day.

An Ode to Joy (of rescuing)
by Will Pollock

*A*mid the sadness of a relationship breakup, I had no idea if I'd see Triscuit again. My soon-to-be ex was on his way to pick her up for the last time.

Those life changes left me feeling gloomy—separating from a human for whom I cared greatly while also saying goodbye to a wonderful, furry creature I adored.

Charley, Triscuit, and I had been through a torrent of activities when we were together: renovation to my home, appearances on two national television shows, and lots of fun travel.

Charley and Triscuit drove away, and that chapter closed. "Let the healing begin," I thought to myself.

Charley rescued Triscuit from the Atlanta Humane Society in 2005. She had acute reactivity to other dogs, which is the type of behavior that can lead to pups being returned, abandoned, or euthanized.

In the months Charley and I were together, Triscuit was either sitting on my lap or generally attached to my hip.

One day, I received a text from Charley that he was bringing Triscuit over. To stay. When they came in, she tore up the stairs, jumped in my lap, and looked at me eagerly. "What are we gonna do now, daddy?" was the message in her eyes.

That reunion with Triscuit kicked off a torrent of life-altering, peak experiences. She became a social media star, was the subject of two books, and traveled with me everywhere.

The transformative power of gratitude moved me from sadness about our breakup to a lasting appreciation for Charley and his decision to let Triscuit live with me.

Triscuit passed away in July 2022. She was a rescue, but in reality, she rescued me—over and over again. And her spirit will endure, largely through the gratitude I'll always feel.

So do not fear, for I am with you; do not be dismayed,
or I am your God. I will strengthen you and help you;
I will uphold you with my righteous right hand.
Isaiah 24:10

Fierce Gratitude
by Tyra Glaze

*A*t the age of twenty-nine, I was diagnosed with Triple-Negative Breast Cancer. A single mother of two young boys ages seven and four, I was an emotional wreck! Yes, I asked the question, "Why me?" But as time passed, that "Why me?" became "Why not me?" When that shift occurred, I knew my journey and my fight would be life changing.

I didn't tell my children because they were too young to understand, and I didn't want them to be sad or worried. I camouflaged "cancer" by staying positive and enjoying life the best I could. My children were my biggest motivation!

I was blessed with my grandmother and my kids' grandmother, who exemplified strength, courage, and hope. They were both diagnosed with breast cancer as well and have passed away. I have many of their qualities, which got me through tough times. I couldn't give up because my sons needed me. I thank God for His grace and mercy. I give Him all the praise!

I've always been strong, but I never knew how strong I really was until I heard the words, "you have breast cancer." I was a FIERCE woman in this FIGHT!

Through chemotherapy, surgery, and radiation treatment, gratitude became my attitude. I WON. Glory to God! I was a WARRIOR. I didn't give up! I'm grateful for the little things in life. Breast cancer was just a chapter in my life, not the whole book!

Nine years later, at thirty-nine, I'm thankful for life. I'm a WARRIOR who's bold, breast-less, beautiful, and blessed! I will continue to share my journey with others to empower and encourage them. Life happens, and we must make the best of "it." I had breast cancer; it didn't have me!

Believe
IN
Yourself

Smile
by Susie Marsh

*T*he value of a smile cannot be underestimated, as it is priceless.

It is your gift of love to you and the world.

From within, if you are feeling sad or down, then the sheer impact on your well-being—if you consciously choose to smile—will shift the dark clouds. It will bring solutions to the challenges that were giving you sadness. This life skill works with feeling overwhelmed, too!

A smile can solve frustration and lead to a better outcome when you want help—and even if it does not, you have done your best to be positive.

The vibration of a smile will lift your spirit. You will exude happiness. You are giving yourself a warm, cheerful hug, lighting up your world, eyes, and body. The additional beauty is that it costs you nothing.

Go on, gift yourself any time, any place, anywhere! Feel the shift deep within you. Others around you will respond with smiles!

You will attract happy people with your aura, joy, and happiness.

Be gifted back by receiving smiles. This will then multiply your internal feelings and vibration, perpetuating more happiness. It can be a never-ending circle of love.

Ask yourself, *would you rather be with someone who is smiling or with someone who is constantly frowning?*

I am grateful I can gift myself right now! I invite you to Smile now. Mother Teresa said, "Every time you smile at someone, it is an action of love, a gift to that person, a beautiful thing." And don't forget the saying, "Smile. You never know who is falling in love with your Smile."

Gratitude makes sense of our past,
brings peace for today,
and creates a vision for tomorrow.
Melody Beattie

The Cancer Cure
by Beth Johnston

"You have advanced cancer" are not words anyone hopes to hear.

After months of healing and rehabbing a broken knee, I was almost relieved to know there was a reason I wasn't feeling like myself. I wasn't just getting older and slowing down!

Surgeries, months of chemo, nausea, hair loss, and brain fog followed. I don't remember everything, but my husband, Mark, does. I think it may have been harder on him than it was on me.

It didn't take long to realize that falling and breaking my knee was God's way of telling me to slow down, take inventory of myself, and take action.

So, I am grateful for that moment when my right knee hit a pile of boxes stacked for "tomorrow's" drop-off at the church, and my left knee met the cold cement basement floor.

I am grateful that a broken knee slowed me down enough to be diagnosed just in time for chemo to be a viable path for me.

I am grateful that I have since been blessed with many "tomorrows." I am grateful to realize that "tomorrows" are never guaranteed. I no longer take them for granted.

Cancer may have been as much a cure in my life as it was a disease; it put so much into proper perspective.

Bad hair days are no longer an issue—I'm just grateful to have hair again.

I am grateful that I don't need to have the last word—I don't think we ever really do!

Most of all, I'm grateful that Mark was my coach, chef, chauffeur, comfort, counselor, and constant reason to exchange a challenging two years of my life for as many more "tomorrows" as possible we may be given—together.

The Day I Accepted Defeat

by Tanner Willms

*L*ife has a funny way of teaching you its toughest lessons and at the worst possible time. For me, it was the day before my son's very first Thanksgiving. I had obtained a vicious drinking problem over the course of a few years, and on the day before Thanksgiving, my wife gave me the choice of going to a rehab facility to better myself or to pack my bags. I was terrified.

The original plan was to go the day after Thanksgiving, but I knew I couldn't make it through the day sober and figured my family was better off I left early. At the time, I was frustrated with a lot of things—my wife for one. I thought I could kick this problem on my own, and who has the money to take that much time off work anyway? How would we pull this one off? Thank God she supported me and loved me enough to push me to go while she stayed back and looked after our son, dogs, and everything around the house during the busiest time of the year. I not only missed my son's first Thanksgiving but also Christmas and the New Year.

I was so down on myself, thinking I was a horrible parent for missing all these big milestones when in reality, it was the exact opposite. I missed my son's first holiday season so that I could truly be there for all the rest of them. I spent 41 days in rehab, and it changed my life forever. I am a better father, husband, and son because of this experience, and I couldn't be more thankful for all the support from my family. One year sober as of Thanksgiving Day 2022.

There are only two ways to live your life.
One is as though nothing is a miracle.
The other is as though everything is a miracle.
Albert Einstein

The Day Everything Changed
by Christopher Rausch

I'll never forget the day when everything normal and certain turned completely upside down and forever changed me as a person. To be honest, I've had more than a few of these days in my life, but I feel called to share this with you now. I'm confident it will provide great inspiration and give you the tools you need to shift your mindset from worrier to warrior.

On May 10, 1982, I became a seventh-grade homeless dropout living in the backseat of a station wagon with my mother and her eighteen cats and four dogs. Over the next four years, I experienced two different moments in my life that brought me to the point of wanting to end it.

Then it all changed. I was introduced to a man who didn't judge me for how I looked or what I'd been through. Instead, he provided suggestions for how I could take full responsibility for my life and change the course of it forever. With his beliefs securely packed in my front pocket, I set out to earn my G.E.D. I then enrolled in college and spent the next twelve years earning my master's. The same year I purchased my first house.

The worst experiences of my life helped me become the man I am today. I've achieved many notable accomplishments in my life. Most importantly, I've learned that life is happening *for* us, not *to* us. When have you grown the most? I'll bet it was when times were challenging.

Focus on where you are *going*, not where you've *been*. Love yourself, ensuring you are surrounded by the best people who push you to be your BEST! Trust me. It's incredible what can change in your life when you do!

Clean Heart
by Noel Vandegraft

*D*riving home today, I couldn't help but take notice of two men walking. My heart sank. I haven't seen these men for seventeen years. As I was driving, I kept staring in my rear-view mirror, looking at a past that once destroyed me.

I parked the car at my childhood home. The same two men I'd noticed were now turning down the street. It was a hot summer day, and both men looked as though life had defeated them. On May 10, 2005, one of these men had been the driver of the car in which my brother was killed. Here I was, seventeen years later, grieving the loss of my brother Adam, having flashbacks to that night and our childhood together. The men that used to come over for dinner were not shamefully walking past my parents' home with their heads down. They walked by as though nothing had happened.

At that moment, I didn't feel anger but forgiveness. I forgave that man, even though he never asked for it. A feeling of relief overwhelmed me. I had waited for this moment for seventeen years. Later that night, I went home and looked up forgiveness in the Bible, and the following scripture gave me clarity. "Create in me a clean heart, O God; and renew a right spirit within me." (Psalm 51:10 KJV) To renew my heart by forgiving in order to heal and to have all the fruits the Lord has in store for me—that's a beautiful thing.

155 M.P.H. Winds Changed Me Forever
by Peggy Willms

L iving through nine hours in the eye of a Category 4 hurricane wasn't on my Bucket List. On September 28, 2022, Hurricane Ian decided to take a sharp right toward us and add himself to my resume of life. The animals, material objects, and landscape have forever changed. I have as well - physically, emotionally, spiritually, and even financially.

In Southwest Florida, planning, prepping, and positioning for natural disasters are the norm. We stock up on pantry items, batteries, and candles. With the expectation of power loss, gas and propane tanks are filled, cash is withdrawn from the bank, and Ziplock bags of water are frozen. Tubs and sinks are filled in case the water shuts off so you can flush toilets and clean up. Shutters are inspected as they will certainly be drawn shut. Piggyback phone chargers are ready to go, flashlights are gathered, and the AM radio is close by.

We had evacuated when Irma, the last Category 4 hurricane, into town. Therefore, Ian was our first "in-home experience." When in the eye of the storm, you are hit twice – on its way over and then as it passes. I will never forget the sounds, smells, and emotions.

After the storm, we flung open the doors and were thrilled to see homes still standing but devastated to see all the debris and flattened trees. There were no visual or auditory sounds of wildlife. As we spent the day checking on neighbors, assessing damages, and cleaning our surroundings, our emotions caught up to us. Being grateful for what God saved is an understatement.

The animal kingdom changed. We found birds that didn't make it. A group of orange-billed, quirky ducks arrived. I wondered if they thought, "Hey, Dorothy, we aren't in Kansas anymore!" Their disorientation was palpable. Yet many of our "regular" visitors, such as my favorite anhinga bird, turtles, alligators, and herons, were gone.

Places and landscapes changed. Sanibel and Pine Island bridges collapsed. Buildings on Ft. Myers Beach were flattened, and many beaches around us were wiped away. The character of those structures will be gone forever as many will be replaced with modern flavors and codes. Trees and other foliage have been ripped to shreds or whisked away altogether. Even mounds of dirt once silencing the interstate traffic have washed away.

People changed. We sat hour by hour, day by day, waiting for power to be reconnected again with the world. Being new to the neighborhood, we were able to meet our wonderful neighbors. Grumpy attitudes and hurriedness dissipated.

Emotional attachment to "things" revealed itself. I don't consider myself a material object girl. Yet, I was affected while watching others hold a broken necklace or smashed candy dish and, conversely, their elation when they found an unharmed photo album.

Animals, places, things, and people have forever changed. I learned how important it is to pencil things into your calendar and not put them off. Explore your surroundings, talk to the birds, sit on the beach you love, or climb a tree as it may be gone the next day. Do not put off a call to a loved one, and respect and treasure your family heirlooms.

I will not say I am grateful for the devastation caused by the storm; I will say the event has taught me lessons, allowed me to appreciate the moments, and I am making new memories.

Reflect upon your present blessings—of which ever man has many—not on your past misfortunes, of which all men have some.

Charles Dickens

Changed from the Inside Out

by Lisa Bianchino

C rushed. Lost. Hopeless. Defeated. Stuck. Confused. Afraid. Invisible. These words defined me during my senior year of college. I can still taste the memory of them. I walked around feeling like I didn't belong anywhere, and something was wrong with me. I wondered what my purpose was and why I existed. Did anyone really care about me? Why didn't anyone understand me? I couldn't figure out how to feel and think differently about myself.

I was not confident I'd ever be free of the heartache and mental and emotional torment. This is where my gratitude story starts. I'm not the same person I was then. I had an encounter with the God of Isaiah 61:1.

Was it easy? No. But was it real? Yes. Has He been the only thing that has ever really changed me from the inside out? Yes.

How does He do it? That's tough to answer in a few words. For me? People. Counselors. Deliverance. Time in His Creation. Journaling. Steps of faith. The purity of the gospel. Self-care. Healthy boundaries. Supportive community. Forgiveness. Other people's stories. Good listeners. A lot of prayer. Writing God's Word on my heart. Taking Him at face value. Taking "healthy risks" instead of "wishful thinking risks." The most important part is that I had to learn how to do all of this—it's a journey.

I share this because it is my own reminder that when we can't see past the fog, can't find our feet to stand on, we're being held. Our faithful God is working out what we simply cannot see.

He has sent me to bind up the brokenhearted,
to proclaim freedom for the captives and release
from darkness for the prisoners.
Isaiah 61:1b NIV

Grateful for the Journey
Anonymous

S mall and simple things make us very grateful for what we have. I'm thankful for taking the time to help my friend to share my experiences. That's how we heal, through other people's past experiences. It's about the little things that help us get where we need to go while helping others along the way. We just never know who needs our help or how they may help us.

I made a choice that should NEVER have been an option, but I let the adversary and negative thoughts get the best of me. It brought me to a place where I did not want to be. A friend helped me out of this darkness into the light by sharing a simple quote. "Don't carry your mistakes around with you. Instead, place them under your feet and use them as steppingstones to rise above them." I kept wondering how I could rise above something totally against God's plan. I know opposition is in all things, and things happen for a reason. I desperately needed to get out of the darkness into the light. That's where God wants us ALL to be. My research brought me on a journey of making new friends through organizations offering healing retreats. Also, let's not forget about the tears, phone calls, and writing my feelings down on paper. I'm so thankful for mentioning this to my friend. I'm so thankful I took the top bunk so that another participant could join the retreat and for those who didn't give up on me.

I'm grateful I kept moving forward, finding the strength I needed to get off the dark and dreary path to find the joy and light I desperately needed. Through the long hard journey, God led me to heal. All thanks to Him!!!

Horses and Harmony
by Ann Marie Lewis

Sometime in my early sixties, I pondered my past and future life. I asked God, "what shall I do until death do I part?" I had a "feeling" I should use my skills as a psychologist certified in EMDR to help our military. For some reason, I kept thinking horses ought to be involved. There had to be a way to combine rescued horses with veterans who have PTSD. Crazy as I had not been involved with horses in over 40 years.

Initially, I was unaware of how to connect horses with EMDR, Eye Movement Desensitization and Reprocessing, but I was confident there was a way. About two weeks later, through my professional mailing list, I found training in Arizona by a woman who combined horses with EMDR.

In June 2014, I met with several local people who understood my vision and were interested in helping form a nonprofit. I met equine specialist Heather Stage, who was knowledgeable about horses. We ultimately worked together for years, helping to form Equines for Freedom.

The following month, I was able to share my story with more people as I set voyage on an Alaskan cruise featuring entertainment from one of my favorite contemporary Christian singers named Michael W. Smith. During that time, I met Mary Eichemeyer, who confirmed my call through prayer. She organized a prayer warrior group comprised of Michael W Smith fans who have prayed for us all these years.

Prayer has been very important to me. I am extremely grateful for God's "call" upon my life, for the prayer warriors, Heather Stage, our Board who worked hard to provide free treatment to veterans, Gary Johnson, who maintains the grounds and builds anything we need, our dedicated treatment team, The Johnson family, who runs a golf tournament for Equines for Freedom and all those who have helped to make the program successful.

Excerpt from "Odyssey through Hell"
by M. Yeró Morris

I have concerns, but I'm happy.
I have problems, but I'm happy.
I have sadness, but I'm happy.
I don't have any money, but I'm happy.
I have angers and frustrations, but I'm happy.
Happiness is a state of being.
It is the light inside us all,
In every little stupid thing,
Usually hidden to the blind-by-will's eye.
Yeah, my stuff, of course, I have nice possessions,
But happiness is beyond that, I'm not stupid.
Happiness is in every morning's butterfly's flyby,
In the wildflower in the middle of the pavement,
Or the broken pot,
In the squirrels in my garden,
Stealing my avocados:
Go on, that's what they are there for!
In the worm that today bites off my flowers.
It will be tomorrow's flyby.
In my dog, her age-illness and her toys.
In my friends and family,
Even the ones that hallucinate me, still love y'all.
In thankful and smiling people,
In my boys and their bikes,
Their fantastic games and jokes,
My own clumsy ones as well,
In the blue or dark sky, Wet or dry, hot or cold,
I do enjoy them all

In hopes and dreams, though stupid they may seem,
Mostly to people who have lost their own.
In that boy who did not write even a kinda-poetry or a kinda-painting in fifteen years.
By the way, I fell on my ass and couldn't stop laughing
Chasing that bubble in the park.
Life IS a constant battle,
But without happiness
Everything turns shadowy gray
Angry to be happy, Angry just 'cause and for all,
Ain't that just sad…and boring?
Happiness lies in smiling at everything in life,
In being thankful.
I will never be bullied or broken ever again
Because…It's just me…being happy…

When one door of happiness closes, another opens;
but often we look so long at the closed door that we
do not see the one which has been opened for us.
Helen Keller

Don't quit yet, the worst moments are usually
followed by the most beautiful silver linings
You have to stay strong, remember to keep your
head up and remain hopeful.
Unknown

Time to Roll Up Our Sleeves
by Mike Starr

I am grateful for my perspective on people. I see folks through a lens of possibility, empathy, and respect. I truly love people for who they are and seek to understand them and their pasts. I believe we all have remarkable potential to heal and promote harmony. We can find a way to have a rewarding and meaningful life built on a foundation of integrity.

I am grateful for Teresa's helping me publish and promote an empowering message. Central to my message is a method to help heal and assist communities and the individuals within them to solve the real challenges we face. Lincoln sought to lead the nation to heal from differences and division after the Civil War when he spoke these famous words during his second inaugural address: "with malice towards none, with charity towards all."

Let us seek common ground and strive to understand one another's talents and imperfections. Let us work together to make peace and progress and to heal. I am grateful to be promoting the good within humanity. I am grateful to all that came before me to make me who I am. I am grateful for the sunshine, hope, growing compassion, and cooperation in the days ahead. Serious problems and crises need attention and remedy today. Now is the time to roll up our sleeves and work together. I am grateful to believe that collectively we will do better…much better.

Small Town Girl with Big Dreams
by Nova Jane E. Alcoran

*T*o be grateful is not always expressed in the form of money. It is about being grateful for how God has given us this life, our life. I am grateful for all things, no matter how small or big they are.

I grew up in a small town in the Philippines called Sapang Dalaga, which means "Young Girls River." When I used to live there, I always wanted to move to a bigger city. Even though I live in a small town, my dream was bigger than any town in the world.

Growing up, we didn't have much. Life was difficult, but I always looked on the bright side. I am grateful that God has given me the eyes to see what really matters. Because I know, with his guidance, life will be colorful and meaningful.
Yes, there will be challenges, but I am grateful for them.

I consider my ups and downs as how grateful I am because they made me realize how to become strong and deal with this kind of situation because I know this will be my fuel to face other circumstances in the future.

And to those who always have my back, guide, help, and teach me good things, they are my guardians. And I am so grateful to have them.

The more that you trust and believe in angels,
the more they will pour their blessings upon you.
Denise Linn

In Gratitude to Our Guardian Angels
by Kathleen O'Keefe-Kanavos

*O*ur Guardian Angels are always with us, but when they answer prayers and requests as insignificant as "Parking Angel, please help!" my gratitude defies words. Thank God for Guardian Angels.

When diagnosed with breast cancer recurrence, I felt alone for an excellent reason; few women survive advanced-stage recurrence. But it did not take long to realize I was never alone; *we* are never alone. We are all born with Guardian Angels. We are their job, and they take that job seriously.

There is only one rule: The Rule of Permission. To receive, you must ask. I learned this Gratitude Lesson while praying for guidance to survive recurrence. My angels heard me and used dreams to share profound healing and nutritional information that guided me to recovery. Because of Angelic intervention, I am alive today to share my story with you.

The Rule of Permission does two crucial things. It does not allow for interference between realms, no matter how noble the action, and ensures that we know what we want.

You may say, "Of course, I know what I want!"

How often have you received "help" from a well-meaning family member, workmate, or friend that was not what you wanted? Perhaps you thought they were interfering while they felt helpful, creating an awkward situation. If only they had asked permission. If only you had expressed exactly what you wanted. The Rule of Permission keeps your angels on track and you in gratitude.

No One Can Stop Me
by Bethany Shaffer

I was born with moderate to severe hearing loss and wore hearing aids until age five. When I was five years old, I got pneumonia and a high fever, leaving me profoundly deaf after recovering. A few months later, I received a cochlear implant.

I attended a mainstream school and unfortunately had to deal with bullying from the other students due to being different. However, I've found over the years that the worst thing about being deaf wasn't my inability to hear without my cochlear implant. People tend to stereotype me and treat me differently due to their perceived limitations regarding my "disability."

I've always found satisfaction in proving them wrong because if I've learned anything in my life, I can do anything I want. The only one that can stop anyone from learning or doing what they want is themselves. I've learned to play musical instruments, including the violin. I played the violin in my middle and high school orchestras. I received my commercial art and design certification when I graduated high school. I received a degree at Keystone College for Fine Arts, where I graduated Cum Laude. I went on to get married after college, and we currently have a dog and three cats. My husband and I have welcomed our daughter, Cecelia, our first child this year. I work formatting books as well as being a freelance artist. The biggest lesson I've learned as a deaf person is that the only one that can stop you is yourself.

And we know that in all things God works for the good of those who love him, who have been called according to his purpose.
Romans 8:28

The Check is in the Mail
by Laura Fleming Summa

*M*y husband and I had been married for a few years and had just bought our first home. We were enjoying a charmed life as artists doing freelance artwork. We got to drink our coffee and work in our pajamas each morning. Life was wonderful! Then one day, while dropping off artwork, my husband was told there would be no more work. The company that we were working for decided to hire another company to acquire any needed artwork. We were abruptly unemployed and couldn't collect unemployment compensation because we were freelance workers. We had bills to pay, and we had no money.

We prayed. My husband contacted the new company and started driving two and a half hours each way to do the same work we had been doing before. We weren't making much money because of the travel time and cost. I got a job as a cake decorator in a local store. It didn't pay very much, but it was something. People from our church helped us. We were so thankful, but we still needed a significant source of income.

We had just both put applications in at a local book bindery. We drove home in silence. I am sure we both wondered where God was in all of this. I was feeling so hopeless. I brought the mail in, and as I shuffled through all of the bills, there was a letter from an attorney addressed to me. I opened it and started reading that my great aunt had named me in her will, and the enclosed $10,000.00 check would be followed by an $8,000.00 check in a few weeks. It was God's timing, and it was both exciting and humbling at the same time. God still performs miracles!

149

HEY LITTLE
fighter
THINGS
WILL GET
Better

Turning Struggles into Opportunities
by Patricia Froehlich

I was the last kid picked to play on every gym class team. Asthma and environmental allergies made exercise torture before inhalers and antihistamines. I fought shortness of breath, burning eyes, and a runny nose, along with symptoms no inhaler or antihistamine could have cured: humiliation and self-doubt. The kids whined, "Do we *have* to have *her* on our team?" and the gym teachers' disdain haunted me for years.

Today I am grateful to those kids and gym teachers because I learned to view struggles as opportunities and to make every member of my team feel welcome.

Working through college as a secretary created the opportunity to become a more focused student. When I became a lawyer, I had the opportunity to treat my support team with dignity and respect instead of asking them to make my tea.

Struggling with law school loans gave me the opportunity to teach at night after working as a prosecutor all day. I am so grateful for those classrooms where I found my public speaking voice and lavished attention upon students who found studying difficult, encouraging them instead of discouraging them.

Struggling with physical challenges gave me the opportunity to meet compassionate healthcare practitioners who encouraged me to develop my strengths, including one astute doctor who suggested I try yoga.

Initial struggles with some of the yoga postures allowed me to deepen my practice and studies. Deepening my practice and studies allowed me to become a yoga teacher, where I utilize my public speaking voice, physical strength, and compassion.

And when a struggle comes at me today, I know I will soon be grateful for an opportunity!

151

He performs wonders that cannot be fathomed,
miracles that cannot be counted.
Job 5:8-9

The Big Honchos Out There
by Sharon E. Martin, MD PhD

I am in tune with the natural world, especially animals. I have two rescued barn cats, two adopted pygmy goats, and one adopted miniature donkey. I live on beautiful land, which is sacred because of the animals. My daily life is rewarded with brays from the donkey or ankle rubs from the barn cat. Abundance has fur, hoofs, and four legs.

Here, I commune with nature spirits and the unseen world. Connecting here gives me a sense of security. I feel at one with the elements, Earth, and galaxy.

However, the cost of being in tune with the animals is that I become unglued if anything is wrong. Buster, my cream and orange barn cat, went missing for a few days. I called and called. This was so unusual. Down the rabbit hole of fear and worry, I went. Is he dead? Did a coyote get him?

My anxiety was paralyzing. I circled the property repeatedly and ultimately told myself sternly to stop. My roundabouts were fruitless. Sitting down at the entrance to the barn, I dug deep, surrendering to higher powers, the greatness that exists outside of me.

Little by little, my breathing slowed. As if bowing to energies larger than me, I called out to the Master Deva of Cats. At least, I intuited that there was one big honcho for the cat world. Bring back my Buster, please. I love him, and I want to know he's safe.

From deep in the barn, out walked Buster, covered with hay and looking sleepy. Gratitude spilled over me. Thank you, Most High Spirit. Thank you, Beings I Cannot See. Thank you for reminding me of the power of connecting to you. All is well.

Letting Go of Resentment
by Janice Silva

*R*eflecting on years ago and where I am now, I am inspired by the growth. I have been in the wellness space for 25 years, so it was very discouraging to find myself lost after an accident in 2009 that caused a ripple effect of destruction and despair. After four surgeries to save my leg and putting on 100-plus pounds, I felt so depressed.

The financial stress of losing everything darn near killed my family and me. It was paralyzing. I needed a healthy reset.

Thankfully, a friend thought enough of me to reach out and share a solution. I began my nutritional rebalancing reset immediately, and within three days, I knew I had finally found the way out!

Addressing nutritional deficiencies gave me the clarity to dream again and make the choices necessary to set goals and reach them. To change my environment and eliminate negativity and guess what? It worked.

I learned to love myself healthy, avoid self-sabotaging behaviors and lean into my transformation. I gratefully released 125 pounds and resentments and developed a healthy relationship with food again, especially with myself, a complete whole-body wellness transformation that started with choosing to change my thoughts.

I started sharing my healthy toolbox and healthy choices and growing a new business out of it while traveling the country for 3 and 1/2 years in our RV. It was a blast! And life changing.

I've been able to create a life I love, travel from our home base in Maui, and pay it forward daily by helping others align with their transformation. There is so much healing in giving back.

It is amazing what happens when you start feeding your mind and body with loving, healthy change.

If you've been in an unhealthy cycle for a long time, there is a way out, and I'm living proof.

We don't inherit the earth from our ancestors,
we borrow it from our children.
Native American proverb

Nature's Dance
by P.J.

*Y*esterday, I sat in a park next to a fairly young tree with long willowy branches gently and freely dancing in—and with—the wind. They were playing together right beside me and kept reaching out, beckoning me to join their dance party.

Their connection was beautiful, tender, elegant, and intimate. The intimacy arose because the wind and tree—very obviously—knew each other. It was apparent they had played together many times before and had a healthy, happy relationship sharing in their joy of movement together.

In that moment, I felt privileged to be in the presence of grace—real grace! Touched and inspired, I shared a smile and a genuine, "Thank you for playing with me and inviting me to join your dance party. I am grateful."

My heart was floating ever so lightly in the soft breeze, playfully dancing in rhythm with my new dance partners—a sapling with the grace and elegance of a prima ballerina and a warm, gentle breeze invisibly lifting and leading me to a truer understanding of real freedom.

Filled with a renewed sense of innocence, my gratitude was both profound and sincere! I was not grateful "for" the experience. I was grateful, specifically, "to" the wind and tree for encouraging and inviting me to dance with them—and for actually playing with me!

Being grateful "to" something or someone invites a deeper humility and creates intimacy between you and the person or thing you are grateful for. Gratitude "for" recognizes and honors the gift. More precisely, it recognizes and honors the value the gift—whether a person, place, or thing—has brought and is currently bringing you. However, you experience and express gratitude, embrace the elegance and beauty it reveals for you!

157

Defy the Status Quo
by Susan Sheppard

*O*K, God, I am ready to move on! If I am supposed to pass on this nursing job and continue my search to be a business consultant, please give me a sign." This is the prayer I spoke as I left the hospital where I had just been offered the position of Trauma Center Coordinator. We were in salary negotiations, and I promised to decide by Monday.

On Monday, the hospital administrator greeted me with, "We have good and bad news. Which would you like first?"

The bad, of course. The hospital board of directors voted over the weekend to close the Trauma Center, and there is no coordinator position. I laughed out loud, said thank you and goodbye to the hospital's good news. God gave me a sign!

It was 1986. I had been an ER nurse since 1964 and had held several middle management positions in various reputable hospitals. I wanted to know if I could do something else. I had just graduated with my Bachelor of Science in business, and I was going to be an entrepreneur. The following week the opportunity to work for Michael Gerber, the renowned small business development coach, materialized, and I was hired as a business development specialist.

Since early childhood, I had defied the status quo, refusing to accept no for an answer and depending on my ability to manifest opportunities. I am grateful for being born who I am, with the courage to step outside my comfort zone and the willingness to act while refusing to settle for less than what I want in every facet of my life. I am widely grateful for my family members, mentors, and incredible learning experiences.

"When we focus on our gratitude, the tide
of disappointment goes out and the
Tide of love rushes in."
Kristin Armstrong

When the Dust Settles
by Tammy Hader

"*Y*ou are surrounded by the Canadian Rockies, and you are taking a picture of a dirt road," my husband remarks with baffled amusement. Teetering between weird and adorable, my actions remind him of why he married me twenty-five years ago.

"A car could pass a combine with room to spare on this luxurious dirt road. I know fellow Kansans who long for what this road has to offer."

A half hour ago we sat in our Airbnb in Canmore, Canada contemplating the advice of strangers for Tuesday's vacation adventure. Paved highway vs. dirt road. Either choice will get us where we want to go, but which one will take us on the most memorable journey. The 742 is a bumpy dirt road, requires slower speeds and is, well … dusty. Highway 40 assures beautiful surroundings and a smoother road to travel. A faster pace will expedite the outing at the potential cost of missing something amazing.

Dirt road it is.

The rented SUV convulses as it propels over the washboard transition from pavement to dirt. We share a hopeful glance at each other, anticipating the reward waiting on the other side of the struggle. Bumps in the road send the SUV fishtailing and jar us out of complacency more than once. Hasty travelers encourage us to pull over to allow them to speed ahead. The luxurious width of the dirt road facilitates this task with ease. The cloud of dust gravitates back to the ground while we linger in the destination of here and now. Nature blesses us with gorgeous lake views, a magnificent valley, big horn sheep, deer, a hoary marmot, and a bear.

I am grateful to forget the world together with him, if only for a moment.

The Surprise Gift
by Al Summa

*I*t is strange how gratitude can manifest itself from negative experiences, and in ways you could never have imagined possible. Months or even years later, these misfortunes sometimes turn into blessings. Never underestimate the power of Faith

When I think of gratitude, my family comes to mind first. My wife and I married and were looking forward to being parents. We both loved children, but it seemed it might never be. We had several miscarriages over eight years; twice it was twins. Heartache was an understatement.

Amid all that heartache, we wondered if we were just not meant to be parents, yet we tried desperately to hang onto a glimmer of hope. "One day…. Maybe." But it was nearly impossible to imagine a happy ending when we were soaked with such sadness.

One day, we received a surprise call asking if we would be interested in adopting a baby. With a failed adoption and all those miscarriages haunting our past, we were cautiously joyful. After eight years, countless doctors, and soul-wrenching heartache, our son was born! We went to the hospital to feed him, and the following day he came home! The excitement and joy were amazing!

We told the doctor stories of other couples who had adopted and had another child in the usual way. He gently said, "That will never be you guys." To our surprise, my wife became pregnant with our beautiful daughter a couple of years later.

Many of us feel lost when sadness fills our days, and we can't see past the present to imagine a happier future. These are the opportunities God uses to show us that he is faithful, always fulfills his promises, and that amazing things can happen. The pain of the past dissolves and is replaced with joy. My daughter is now expecting her first child, our first grandchild, any day. That is truly something to be thankful for.

163

"Family and friends are hidden treasures,
seek them and enjoy their riches."
Wanda Hope Carter

Our Son's Prayer
by Jacki Long

*A*fter my husband and I lost our second baby, I gave up the dream of having another child. Instead, we focused on recovering from our devastation and navigating through intense grief. Our priorities shifted. We made changes in our careers and removed our son from childcare.

My husband and I eventually attempted to expand our family again. We tried for two years, enduring monthly disappointments. I was convinced we would remain a three-person family. It had been so easy to get pregnant before, but it wasn't happening now.

Our son regularly asked for a baby sister. I would answer, "It's up to God."

"Please, God. Please bring me a baby sister," my son begged.

He wasn't exactly the praying kind of kid. But when he prayed for his lost pets to come home, we heard their cries within seconds after his prayer.

After he started kindergarten, I decided I was "OK" without starting over with a newborn. I convinced myself I was OK to avoid the painful reality that we would not have another baby.

My husband and I agreed that it wasn't meant to be. We decided to schedule a permanent procedure, ending our chances of pregnancy forever. I was "late" by two days, which was common, but I took a test to be sure. Expecting yet another letdown, I watched the formation of an ever-so-faint test result line indicating pregnancy!

Nine months later, we had our miracle—a healthy baby girl. Our son's plea was answered. I learned not to underestimate the power of prayer. When I keep my eyes open, and heart expanded, I find answers. Today, widowed from their father, I marvel at our adult kids—and am reminded of their daddy and my husband.

165

Endings Can Be Amazing Gifts
by Ilene Gottlieb

We met in college as part of a group activity, typical for 1973. He was interested in my roommate, not me. I don't remember how his attention shifted to me, but we married after dating for three years. I was 23, and he was 25. In our first year of marriage, we spent only every third night and weekend together. He was my priority, and this was my joy.

For 11 years, we shared a life that would have seemed ideal for many, but we weren't happy. Was being happy in a marriage what was important? He requested a divorce, and I was devastated. Nine years later, after my spiritual awakening, I searched for him to close the circle and say, "thank you."

At that time, I was beginning to understand the healing qualities of the energy of Gratitude. My most pivotal healing moment was a phone conversation where we shared, laughed, and cried, and I thanked him for having the strength to request a divorce when I could not.

Without this heartbreaking experience, I would not BE who I am today, affectionately known as "The Heart Healer." The thousands of beautiful people whose lives I have been blessed to touch from around the world would never have happened.

Gratitude is necessary to shift one's focus from being a victim to being empowered. I often hear myself saying, "It's all good; it just doesn't always feel good." Gratitude and Love for every blessed moment of life open incredible doors to healing.

Years later, Ho'oponopono, the ancient Hawaiian problem-solving process, came to me and has become a primary focus for how I serve. I find it fitting that the original four phrases of this beautiful process are "I love you, I'm sorry, Please forgive me, and Thank you."

"It is not enough to have lived. We should be determined to live for something."
Winston Churchill

God Set My Purpose on Fire
by Jacquel Tucker

I had a remarkable career in the hospitality industry. I made an excellent salary plus bonuses, traveled to wonderful places, and bought whatever I wanted. I even thought I gave back to others.

But God called me to walk in my true purpose, and everything changed.

I started a non-profit and also became an entrepreneur. Little did I know the sacrifices I would make. With a mission to transform rural schools and communities in Jamaica and serve lower-income families in the USA, my non-profit started growing immediately and took a lot of attention away from my new business. I was doing this work without pay.

I could no longer afford the things I was accustomed to. I was way out of my comfort zone and comfortable lifestyle. I would have been tempted to return to the corporate hamster wheel if not for the fact that serving the less fortunate brought me more joy and fulfillment than anything I had ever done.

During the pandemic, my non-profit served up to 2,000 families per month in Georgia and over ten communities in Jamaica. When I was a young girl growing up in rural Jamaica, we could barely afford our dinner. Now I saw God do the impossible as we sponsored forty students for the school year and provided healthcare for nearly 2,500 residents. We are now getting ready to start construction on our first rural community center in Jamaica!

The sacrifices were great, but it has been worth it. It's made my marriage stronger, my faith and trust in God has exploded, He has set My Purpose on Fire and through my coaching program, I am now successfully helping others do the same by launching their own business or non-profit! I hope you are inspired to take the leap of faith today and do what God calls you to do. I'm already cheering you on!

169

Choose Wisely Mama
by Jes Caroline

*C*hoose family dinner over sports practice and silence over noise.

Choose talking over television and creativity over toys.

Choose intentional over "on-the-go."

Explore books and recipes and be present as they grow.

Choose simplicity, and don't make plans.

Take walks instead of pictures—ditch your phones and hold their hands.

Reject the pull to be busy; it's easy to let stuff fill the day.

Instead of keeping them on schedule, teach them how to pray.

At first, the days seem long, but the minutes start moving fast.

The world tells us to "keep busy," but many look longingly at the past.

Don't let this time slip through your fingers with daily plans and schedules.

Make the messes and take your time because this season is not here to stay.

Learn that doing "more" doesn't make you better.

Free yourself from plans and be an influence your child will remember.

One touch of nature makes the whole world kin.
William Shakespeare

Deeper into Gratitude

by Deborah Beauvais

*E*ach morning, I consciously lie in gratitude while softly awakening. I see my aura as energy dancing around the periphery of my body. As an intuitive, I often play with this energy, moving it all around. I have created a healing ritual acquired from my training and several offerings from other practitioners. I love adding different applications to my healing repertoire.

I have come a long way from the victim held tightly within my little inner child. Gratitude has replaced fear. Some days, gratitude and love must overcome the sadness left by so much loss. But those days are fewer as I fill up with gratitude for my experiences. Deeper gratitude brings more knowledge and spiritual understanding, so I see the gift in the heartache. When ready, I can direct my mind to believe that I am free of the past so I may live in the present, where life's nectar awaits. It becomes a choice—which I would rather experience.

My blessings include a soft, warm breeze gently caressing my face, a voice that directs me away from danger, a hummingbird hovering right in front of my face, and experiencing my late husband's energy as if he was right here. Each one drops me to my knees. Recently, a tiny baby frog hopped into my kitchen at the beginning of a two-month challenge. To my delight, this was followed by another tiny frog at the close of the challenge. Fascinating indeed! It is at these times that I tingle and thank God for the opportunity to feel so much joy on any given day. I am blessed, honored, and grateful to have this earthly experience.

Everyday IS A Fresh START

Standing Still in the Moment

by Sharlene R. Prince

*T*he defining moment came when I realized that despite all my experiences and painful tragedies, I was still standing. So many times, I had complained about what was done to me. I never fully recognized that my life could have been over. After all that I had endured and suffered, by the grace of God, I managed to survive.

I remember driving home one evening from a class that ended at ten pm. I was nearing a very busy intersection in Florida when my brakes gave out. I witnessed all the oncoming traffic as I started to go through the red light. Fear took over my body, and I began to pray to God for help. A voice told me to turn right and aim for the big metal pole. I swiftly turned right to hit the light pole. My life literally flashed before my eyes as I talked to my Lord and Savior. It was like an out-of-body experience, and I heard a loud sound as my airbag exploded, hitting my chest. My car was totaled, and my chest felt like it was on fire.

I sat in my car, stunned, as other drivers approached me and asked if I was okay. The police arrived. I told them my brakes had stopped working, and I shared how I turned to hit the pole to avoid crashing into oncoming traffic. Everyone agreed that was a smart thing to do and said I was lucky to be alive. It was not luck—it was God's intervention. He saved my life. I am so thankful to have God in my life as He forever changed my whole world that day.

175

"How strange that nature does not knock,
and yet does not intrude!"
Emily Dickinson

When a Visitor Changes Your Perspective

by Rene Kamstra

When my marriage ended in divorce, it was difficult. And I knew that I needed to do something to conquer my loneliness. Crying through operas by myself and dining alone weren't enough. With a leap, I scheduled a world tour. Why not – tackle inner work and get to know the real me and how I wanted to move forward?

After four months of traveling, I woke up in Thailand feeling very alone. Although I had a speaking engagement in Fiji for the following week, booking a ticket to return home and see my kids was at the forefront. Something I always tell my clients popped into my head. "Don't make any decision when you are in a negative emotional state."

I set my phone alarm for a thirty-minute sulk session; When my alarm went off, I was still crying, and to be very blunt, snot was dripping. I climbed out of bed, get dressed, and walked to my favorite breakfast restaurant. I sat outside because it was beautiful with lots of plants. Then a miracle happened.

Suddenly, this butterfly came to sit right next to me on the plant. I ordered a beautiful omelet with ham and cheese, and I was waiting for that. As soon as my omelet arrived, the butterfly flew right into my plate, facing outward. Suddenly, it turned around facing inward, started walking, and sat in the middle of my omelet, spreading its wings.

I realized the butterfly was there to give me a message. It was a mesmerizing moment, bringing me fully into the present. I decided to post a story about my visitor on Facebook, asking friends for their opinion, and within one hour, I received 169 messages. That experience taught me that whether I am sad or lonely, with people or not, I am never alone.

never STOP looking UP

That's Faith
by Mark O'Brien

I once stopped in a Starbucks in Albany, New York.

The woman in front of me in line had thick, wavy, dark brown hair, barely streaked with strands of white. She wore a cardigan that matched her hair and a button that said, "Breast cancer: Say it. Fight it. Damn it." Her eyes were radiant. Her smile was luminous.

She said, "Well, hello!" as if her only reason for being there was to greet me.

In her amazing presence, all I could do was ask, "Why do I have the feeling you're so much more alive than I am?"

She then told me about her cancer diagnosis, the support of her husband and children, the professionalism and compassion of her medical team, and her belief in God.

Then she pointed at her hair and said, "God even gave me this. Before chemo, my hair was thin and straight. Now it's thick and wavy. That's a gift."

Her name was Lisa May. Within her energy field, I felt like a battery being recharged, like a sponge absorbing light. We talked for 10 minutes or so. Then her coffee was up. She took it, said goodbye, and left.

A moment later, coffee in hand, I headed out the door. To my right, I saw Lisa getting into her car. I ran to catch her before she left.

I said, a little haltingly: "Do you know how things happen sometimes, and you get the distinct sense they're supposed to happen?"

She smiled and said, "Yes."

Heaven for Mom
by Monica Talbot-Kerkes

$\mathcal{M}$om-
I know you're in Heaven
Holding Mary's hand
Together you walk gently
Through this wonderland

Light is bright upon your face
Tousled in your hair
There is no better place to be
God's love is in the air

You sit beside Jesus
Under stars alive
Moonlight shines upon you
Peace is in your eyes

Heaven is like a rainbow
Swirling in the seas
Beyond our sight and universe
Afar all galaxies

In Heaven, there are angels
Of all spirits gifted there
They promise to protect us
And listen to our prayers

Oh-there really is another world
For a mother just like you
Why else does my heart just burst?
As sweet memories floodeth through

A Fair Soul never dies
That is surely you
The love you gave me dearly shows
Heaven is pure and true

So, I must take heart and trust
That this life is not in vain
Because all of Heaven's beauty
Is worth all of Earth's pain

There is a paradise called Heaven
Amazing, wild, and free
Its winds are your soft kisses, Mom
Now blowing down on me

Thus, I need not be afraid
But look for Heaven's Sun
In it your arms are open wide
And into them, I will run

Joy is the serious business of heaven.
C. S. Lewis

Life Goes On
by Faith Pearce

*A*s I sat watching the balls run down the alleyway, hurtling towards the skittles, my dad walked towards me with a pint of blackcurrant and water. He sat with me for a few minutes, and we chatted about my day and school. Little did I know this would be the last time we would ever speak. At the end of the evening, my mum called me to say it was time to leave. "Wait," I said, "but I haven't said goodbye!" Don't worry. You will see him at home soon."

But fate had other ideas. We waited, but the knock on the door came from two police officers. On my dad's way home, he was hit by a car and knocked off his bike. He never regained consciousness and after two days, we sadly decided to turn off life support due to no brain activity. As he was a young, healthy male, one of the questions they asked was, would we like to donate his organs? After discussion, we all agreed we would.

The next few days and weeks were a blur. But then, in the post, we received the news. Four people had received transplant organs. Although in intensive care, a 57-year-old lady with liver failure was progressing well. A 54-year-old man and a 30-year-old lady both received kidney transplants. Also, a 4-week-old baby received his heart valve.

We received touching letters of gratitude. The recipients could now play with their grandchildren and live a life they hadn't for many years. They said they would remember us every day and be thankful for the gift they had been given.

Four people were given a chance to live. Even though this was one of the most tragic events, I am grateful that part of my dad lives on.

And now these three remain: faith, hope, and love.
But the greatest of these is love.
1 Corinthians 13:13

Grateful to Be a Mother
by Jes Caroline

*M*y children make me see magic in a dandelion and music in a feather.

The dirt between their toes gives me more joy than a chest of jewels.

And they teach me that rocks and shells can be a treasure.

They show me that chalk can build anything, big or small.

And mud can make a potion.

I've learned that if I let them have the freedom to explore their world.

They can accomplish more in a day than all my plans in a lifetime.

Today they sailed as pirates to South America and back again.

And made a restaurant with sand cakes.

The Layered Sky
by Tammy Hader

*M*y quiet spec of fleshy mundaneness sits behind the steering wheel of my orange Honda Fit as I speed down a familiar stretch of highway. The repetitive loop of adulthood traps me between necessity and desire. My glance flows through each layer of the sky as I travel over the speed limit in an act of tempered rebellion not egregious enough to be on anyone's radar.

The gradient backdrop behind the clouds begins as a hopeful cerulean blue. Following the curvature of the sky down to the earth's horizon, the atmosphere degrades into a weary grayness. Near me, the sparse pillowy white clouds with dark gray bottoms offer a version of both hope and despair. Between the puffy perspective floating outside my windshield and the gradient background in the distance, dense clouds form the striated cross-section of the sky's layered geography.

Like an ant below the heavens, I have never felt smaller.

Mom thinks I travel this familiar highway to her home out of obligation for her having birthed me. Obligation is only a tiny sliver of why I do what I do. Her gift of life has now evolved into a gift of purpose for me. I do not care for Mom just because I love her. I like her, too. She is my friend as much as she is family. The sky reminds me of my diminutive place in the grand scale of life. Mom reminds me of gratitude for the people with whom I share my anthill.

I feel a little less small when I am with her.

Your mind, emotions and body are instruments
and the way you align and tune them
determines how well you play life.
Harbhajan Singh Yogi

Morning Awakens
by Susie Marsh

*T*he sun peaks its bright head over the sea's horizon, filling my world with light and possibility for the day ahead. My morning journey begins, like a meditation.

I am grateful for the wonderful sleep I have had, filling me with energy and anticipation for the day ahead. *Thank you. Thank you, universe, for another day in my life.*

This little prayer of gratitude enables me to find the joy and happiness that follows as if by magic. I ask the universe to fill my day.

This leads to the intentions for the day. I know I will have to work, but it always helps to focus on setting the intention of three to five goals to be achieved—all in different life areas. I write my goal list for the day.

I will exercise both my body and mind.

I will nourish my being with good food and water.

I concentrate on breathing in, to let the energy in, then with the following out-breath, I release the fear that pops up.

I now forgive myself for fears or mistakes. I ask, "What can I learn?" It may be as simple as procrastination blocking my achievements. Recognizing and naming the fear leads to gratitude. Today is a new day with fresh possibilities.

I forgive myself for allowing others to have a negative impact on me. I take the lesson to hold the boundary to protect myself.
I love myself for three reasons, breathing in the love and light, then holding the love in my safe place on the outbreath. I Smile. I can now live the day from a place of gratitude and awareness. I appreciate where I live, my strengths, my mind and my body. I know I can overcome whatever challenges the universe puts before me today.

From Mothering None to Mothering Many
by Lisa Caroglanian Dorazio

*H*ave you ever lost or known someone who lost a child? Conceivably you have witnessed inconsolable grief. Can grief really be cured in time? Not all people process loss using the 1969 Elisabeth Kübler-Ross model for grief, nor are all losses the same. They can be overcome.

Giving one direction and a sense of purpose to move forward positively in life is achievable. Yes, by simply engaging in a daily gratitude practice, you, too, can affirm your time, talent, and treasures to make a difference in someone's life.

Becoming proficient in loss management is as simple as implementing three daily gratitude habits: prayer, reading, and writing.

Before getting out of bed, thank the good Lord for what you have experienced, the lessons learned, and the unknown facing you.

Reading positive and hopeful material – messages and stories – to support fundamental beliefs that everything in life has meaning.

Finally, write a note or send a card to the first person that comes to mind. Share with them a heartfelt emotion.

Daily affirmations of anger, depression, denial, bargaining, and even final acceptance served me well. It provided a release opening my heart and mind to others. Ultimately, I accepted the multiple miscarriages I encountered from 1996-1999. It allowed me to reconcile my past. I could look to the future as a grand opportunity to mother many in a different way. Be masterful daily by centering yourself, freeing your mind and heart to liberate yourself from loss.

*Be strong and courageous; do not be frightened
and do not be dismayed, for the
Lord your God is with you wherever you go.*
Joshua 1:9

Gratitude is a Testimony
by Dr. Sally Adukwu-Bolujoko

G ratitude is being thankful and the readiness to show appreciation for a favour received. Societies worldwide socialize their children to appreciate help rendered or compliments expressed. Thank you, therefore, is a common phrase in many languages that conveys gratitude and courtesy.

An African adage says, "the child who is grateful for yesterday's blessing will receive another." It is evident that people who say "Thank you" experience more blessings and favours from God and man. We thank God not just because he has done a lot for us but to open doors for what he will do. Some people lose their blessings and opportunities because they are ungrateful. They lose the support of God and men because they do not show gratitude by saying, "Thank you." Those who constantly remember God's mercies always receive more and blessings overflow in their lives.

With the eyes of faith, we can look beyond our circumstances and be grateful for where we are. This act of faith expresses our hope and trust in God for things we may not see but believe to be true and will manifest. Genuine gratitude is an act of hope and testimony. Remembering God's mercies will help us develop a mountain-moving faith. In Mark 11:22-23, Jesus said that if we have faith like a mustard seed, we can command the mountains, and they will obey. God does not change, as we can see in Malachi 3:6, where he said, "For I am the Lord, I change not." And Hebrews 13:8 says Jesus Christ is the same yesterday, today, and forever.

Consequently, gratitude guarantees that we continue to overcome challenges through the words of our testimonies (Revelation 12:11). David gave testimonies of God's help he received in the bush while tending his father's sheep. He told king Saul about the victories he had and concluded, "The Lord that delivered me out of the paw of the lion, and out of the paw of the bear will deliver me out of the hand of this Philistine" (1 Samuel 17:37). And God delivered him.

Ultimately, being thankful guarantees more blessings. It is a positive trait common in successful people and leaders who are humble, courageous, and people-oriented. It behooves us to pass on this trait to the next generation.

193

Three Steps to Freedom
by Alicia Paz

*B*ecause of domestic violence, I felt unworthy of being loved or cared for. I thought I was human garbage and decided to commit suicide to correct the error the Universe made by wasting energy on me. While writing the suicide note, I thought, "What if? What if there is another way? What if there's a better way? What if the excruciating pain I have gone through could prevent someone else from reaching the same decision of committing suicide?"

In the middle of so much pain, I felt a tiny thread of hope. I felt grateful for feeling that; I grabbed it and developed the practice of Gratefulness, of looking for reasons to be Thankful for and Celebrate.

It was raining, and I thought, "Rain can be depressing. If I could not see the rain, how would I feel?" This is how I discovered the power of gratitude and my freedom to choose my thoughts, one thought at a time.

Since then, I have focused on finding reasons to be thankful every time something happens or if nothing happens. For example, if it's raining, instead of thinking it's sad, I focus on: "I'm so thankful I have eyes, and they work well - I can see the rain! Yippie!"

I used to have panic attacks in traffic. By practicing gratitude, I now enjoy every ride. I thank every part of the car for working well, and I thank and celebrate every part of my body for allowing me to drive.

I summarize this practice with three steps to Enjoy Feeling The acronym is ADAPTC. It is formed by the letters that are underlined:

A: I Acknowledge I am Awakening
D: Step 1. I Deserve Freedom
AP: Step 2. I Accept and Permit Freedom in my life
TC: Step 3. I am Thankful for _____ and I
      Celebrate Freedom in my life.

The word Freedom is changed to Peace, Love, and others in the Journey of Awakening. #iSmileFromMyHeart.

195

6 Habits of Highly Grateful People
by Tasha Chen

F or a long time, the only gratitude I practiced was the stuff
I learned as a kid: to pray with thankfulness over our food,
pray at night for our day, or pray at church on Sundays.

I wanted more - profound gratitude. The type of gratitude that
can drop you to your knees, make you cry, or take your breath
away. I recently dedicated a whole month to harnessing the
principles of gratitude.

I was never raised with a very deep understanding of how to be
grateful, what it looked like, or how to practice gratitude until I
started living what we call, 'the certain way.' Focusing on personal
development, universal principles, and the law of attraction, I
began designing and embracing six gratitude principles.
Embracing them, let's say, didn't happen overnight.

Six Habits of Highly Grateful People:

1) Turn an obstacle into an opportunity, a loss into a gain. Look
   beyond dwelling on negative emotions and circumstances.
2) Manifest with speed. I am not talking about run-of-the-mill
   gratitude. This is another level, higher, more intense. The more
   grateful you are for the good things, the more quickly good
   things will come.
3) Make life happier. Live to create experiences that bring joy. Live
   to create experiences that amplify things to be grateful for.
4) Achieve a deeper level of attunement to the present moment.
   People want to be heard and understood; listen. Be present in
   the most mundane things, whether drinking coffee, at the gym
   or doing something you don't love, like running.

5) Have faith. Knowing that no matter what, it's going to work is true faith. Faith is born out of gratitude. The more you fixate on gratitude, the more faith you develop, which creates more to be grateful for. So, if you had a powerful desire for something, and you were always in crazy faith, like unmatched faith, like nine and a half, nine and three quarters out of 10, you're always in that type of faith. Just think how quickly you would manifest.

6) Practice thanking people. Be more grateful for people than things. It's not just the beautiful, green-inked pen to be grateful for, but taking a moment and thinking about the people that go to work every day who take time away from their family to make the unique color ink and the little shell on the outside of it. Gratitude is more than a pen.

Lastly, thank outside the box. Amplify your gratitude practice. Write at least three things you're grateful for every day for thirty days, and do not repeat anything. So, if yesterday you were grateful for the food in your refrigerator, the electricity that you have AC or heat running in your house, you can't say that again for the next thirty days. Seeing how many things you overlook that you can be grateful for is one of the most powerful activities you can do. I promise you that people with the level of success you desire are practicing these habits of gratitude.

I once looked at the cup half empty and steeped in negative thoughts. It felt awful. I knew I was diminishing my power to create the things that I wanted in my life. Looking at the cup as half full implies not struggling for lengthy periods with negative thoughts, disbelief, or a lack of belief. I am grateful my cup is overflowing with gratitude

For everyone who asks receives;
those who seek find;
and to those who knock,
the door will be opened.
Matthew 7:8

Thanking God for Nothing Yet Everything
by Jane McCarter-Caponigro

G ratitude is something that I used to struggle with. I was the type that thought the glass was half empty until one day, I heard someone say, "Every morning I wake up, I thank God for nothing."

Before I heard the rest of the sentence, I thought, oh my, you have so much to be grateful for... my old personality would usually chime in with, "yes, I know what you mean," but that morning was a turning point for me.

When they finished their sentence, they said," I am Grateful that nothing terrible happened last night. I woke up; I didn't stop breathing, my children are safe and healthy, and I have a roof over my head."

Before long, I was saying how grateful I was. I am grateful for all that they said and so much more. I am grateful that I have children to
love and that they love me.

I can hear them say that they love me, I am thankful that I get to work, I'm healthy, I have food on the table, blessed
friendships, either new or old, and a car that gets me around. I'm able to see the beauty of nature that is all around us.

I'm so grateful God is in my life. He constantly shows me signs that he is near me when I am struggling. I know that gratitude is something that you have to practice every day. Don't let the negative thoughts take up space in your mind or body. And I always remember that God blesses us with another day to start all over again.

When I feel grateful- gratitude, I want to pass it on, even if I tell the cashier that they have a beautiful smile or lovely eyes or help someone carry their bags from the store, tell the sales clerk I appreciate all their help, and give the mail person a bottle of water to show my appreciation. It is hard to think of disappointments when I have a grateful heart.

Gratitude Will Take You Through It
by Teresa Velardi

*I*n this ever-changing world, filled with so many challenges and unknowns, it's essential to keep our minds open and ready to receive goodness and all things positive. Living in gratitude will help you find the way through whatever is before you.

It's been said that "What we think about, we bring about." If you live with an abundance mindset, you will live an abundant life, and there will always be enough. If you live with a scarcity mindset, there will never be enough, no matter how much you have. It's really up to you. We each get one go-'round with this life. How will you choose to go through what shows up? By the way, it doesn't just show up; you manifest it. Remember, what you think about, you bring about. I've had multiple lessons in that.

I often say, "Gratitude is the key that unlocks the door to prosperity in every area of your life." Prosperity is not just about money. It's about goodness in all areas of life:

- Physical
- Emotional
- Relational
- Spiritual
- Financial

Finding gratitude in these areas will improve your life in many ways. You'll always have enough, and because you are grateful, life will give you more!

Do you keep a gratitude journal? I challenge you to start one. Make it fun with something like the "letter of the day" by writing down three things that begin with the same letter. This will help you to look for things and people to be grateful for. This is one way to keep from getting into a rut. Recognizing the same things every day is not a full expression of gratitude.

Gratitude is something you *feel*, not just something you say. The "feeling" part is key to living abundantly. Stepping outside the "box" will expand your life and give you more to be grateful for!

Can you dig deep into your heart and find something to be grateful for, even when you think there is *nothing* to be grateful for? If you rolled your eyes at that one, let me acknowledge you for your honesty. I know from experience that it's sometimes tough to find even one thing to be grateful for when you're in the middle of something you wouldn't wish on anyone. I know it's easier to get through *any* situation when you *can* find something to be grateful for. Believe it or not, quite often, in the end, you will even be thankful for that challenging experience, especially when you realize that your grateful heart carried you through and made the storm a bit easier to weather while opening the door for goodness to follow.

Do you have a story like that? I encourage you to think about it and write it down. In the meantime, grow your gratitude muscles. Make your grateful heart a focal point of day-to-day living, and you'll notice the blessings before you know it.

Contributing Authors

Abby Krietler Hand is a Preconception Health Consultant, who helps women and couples prepare for pregnancy through lifestyle change and health optimization. She holds her Master's in Nursing and is certified in both Epigenetic and Functional Medicine health coaching. Abby is happiest tromping around in the woods looking at plants.

Alan Jude Summa is an internationally published illustrator & author. He began drawing at age two and never stopped. Alan has two children and lives in Poconos with his wife, Laura, two cats, two dogs, and a lizard named, Doc. When not working, he loves to travel and restore vintage motorcycles.

Alicia Paz a Master Freedom Coach®, a Bilingual Physician, Trauma and Addictions Specialist, bestselling international author, senior consultant, storyteller, and speaker with 20+ years' experience in transformational leadership. She has lectured in universities on several continents and teaches people to Enjoy Freedom, One Smile at a time®. TheBestProfits.com.

Alison Treat is the author of the novel, *One Traveler*. She works as a freelance editor and hosts the podcast, "Historical Fiction: Unpacked." When she's not writing, Alison can be found hiking or skiing with her husband and three children in Northeastern Pennsylvania. Learn more at her website, alisontreat.com.

Aljon Comahig, aka Aljon Inertia, creates beautiful, one-of-a-kind illustrations for children's books that speak to good morals and values while providing lessons for today's youth. The illustrations bring engagement to the content, so the story comes alive on the pages. Aljon resides in the Philippines, and his work is seen worldwide.

Alysia Lyons is a mom, entrepreneur, life coach and author. She is passionate about helping women live their lives with more joy, from the inside out. As a certified Master Neuro-Transformational Life Coach, Alysia guides her clients to emotional freedom. Her blog, the Mom Support Coach, focuses on lessons she learns in daily life.

Andee Scarantino is an author as well as a mindset and transformational coach specializing in identity work. She is the creator of getthefuckoff.com and host of The Get the F*ck Off Podcast. Andee holds a Master's Degree in Sociology from Columbia University. Her work incorporates how macro-level systems contribute to individual arrested development.

Angi Currier is a hospital Patient Access Representative and floor manager for a hardware/lumber company. She is a contributing author in the book, *The Four-Fold Formula*. She is a recovered substance abuse addict and knows what it is like to feel alone. Her experience allows her to help others.

Ann Marie Lewis, MA, Pennsylvania Licensed Psychologist is certified in EMDR. Trained in Equine Assisted EMDR and Clinical Coordinator of Equine4s for Freedom. In private practice for 37 years, she helped form Equines for Freedom in February 2015. Ann Marie spends her days treating patients in Clarks Summit, Pennsylvania and working at Equines for Freedom.

Dr. Anne Worth is a Christian author, counselor, and speaker. She has a mother's heart and has "adopted" children from all over the world, some are the four-legged kind. Her books include *"Call me Worthy"* and a series of three children's books entitled *"Tessie's Tears."* Anne is 80 years young.

Beth Johnston is the oldest daughter in a large family; Beth Johnston was born into management! Beth has spent her professional years reorganizing existing companies using her practical and logical perspectives to help companies achieve their highest profit years. She is known for her keen listening skills and inspiring interview techniques, now shared on B.E.P. TALKS. Beth can be reached at info@beptalks.com.

Bethany Shaffer is married to Brian Shaffer and resides in Pennsylvania with their dog, Bailey, and their three cats, Master Henry Squiggs, Gizmo, and Mew. Bethany and her husband, Brian, are expecting their first child soon. Bethany enjoys doing her art and renovating her house in her free time.

A Daily Gift of Gratitude

Christopher Rausch is debatably the world's most effective and impactful UNSTOPPABLE 'No Excuses' coach, speaker, workshop facilitator, retreat leader whose life apprenticeship of the victim to victor is nothing short of miraculous and surely inspiring! www.NoExcusesCoach.com

Colette Srebro Hughes graduated summa cum laude from Keystone College with an Associate Degree in Written Communications. She is best known for her faith, energetic personality, and quirky sense of humor. Her mantra is "Politics and humor may collide, but heaven rules."

Cyndi Wilkins is a certified massage and bodywork professional with a passion for writing/blogging and blazing new trails of thinking. Her approach to healing is recognizing the mind and body function as ONE. She shares her stories as a featured contributor for *Bizcatalyst 360*, blogs for *All Things Wellness*, and a contributing author in *The Four-Fold Formula*.

Dalia Ramahi is an ADR script writer and bilingual, voiceover actress who records characters for video games, animation, K-12 education, audiobooks, mobile apps, and more. She's also known as the joy advocate, because she believes everybody deserves to tap into a life that brings them joy. Learn more at DaliaRamahi.com.

Debara Bruhn Towt, host "The Second Genesis Awakenings" is heard on DreamVision7 Radio Network every Monday and Tuesday at 12am/12pm EST, playing on the Sustainable Living Platform. We explore what it is to embrace the Vast and Infinitely Creative inside us. Human Existence is Fundamentally a Phenomenal Life meant to be shared.

Deborah Beauvais is founder and owner of the Dreamvisions7 Radio Network, a global Holistic Boston-based syndicated Internet Radio Station created in 2007 with a vision to consciously serve humanity. She is an intuitive, healer and Reconnective Healing™ and The Reconnection™ practitioner. Deborah created the Kids 4 Love Project and published her first children's book, *The Paper Doll Kids*.

Debra Costanzo founded 3 in 1 Fitness by D. L. Costanzo, LLC in July 2008. Certified through the Institute of Integrative Nutrition, she loves coaching busy professionals and supporting them to embrace mindful lifestyle changes resulting in better health and sustained energy. Debra resides in Charlotte, NC. debracostanzo@3in1fitness.com https://dcostanzo.juiceplus.com

Diane Simard was named an inaugural Top 100 National Woman in Business to Watch. She is a survivor of Stage III breast cancer, a psycho-oncology influencer, and founder of the Center for Oncology Psychology Excellence. She authored *The Unlikely Gift of Breast Cancer*, one of Book Authority's best breast cancer books.

Dianne Stephens completed her studies at Nova Scotia's Dalhousie University in respiratory therapy. She moved to St. John's, Newfoundland to work in a pediatric and neonatal intensive care setting which also included air ambulance transports. She has spent 25 years in the pharmaceutical industry managing global research trials for new medicines. She is dedicated to personal development and building network marketing businesses.

Dickie-Lee Tran is a Reiki master, and intuitive. She is the 6th generation of healers and loves what she does. Dickie-Lee was born and raised on the island of Maui and moved to California in the year 2000.

Newly published author, Donna Guary, is committed to capturing everyday moments. Out of these moments, gratitude is born and God's plan is revealed. The mother of two adult sons, grandmother, and great-grandmother, Donna is also a graduate of Mid-America Christian University, Air Force veteran, and women's Bible study leader.

Eileen Bild is CEO of Ordinary to Extraordinary Life/OTEL Universe, Executive Director, Founder of The Core Thinking Blueprint Method, OTEL TALK show host, Breakthrough S.P.A.R.K. Coach, Published Author and Internationally Syndicated Columnist. She specializes in Mastering the Inner Game and creating a Framework for Success. coach@eileenbild.com   www.corethinkingblueprint.com
www.oteluniverse.com

205

Emily Manuel lives on the island of Kauai in Hawaii where she is a realtor and owns a fogging and disinfecting company. Very active in serving her community Emily uses her solution finding skills, positive attitude, and energy to encourage others to work hard and succeed. Emily desires to share her knowledge with others.

Erica Lewis is a dance enthusiast and recovering attorney. By day, she works at a corporate law firm and by night, she indulges her passions of dance and languages. She is a lifelong learner who loves a good laugh and a good story. Erica has degrees from Barnard College, Columbia University and Harvard Law School.

Faith Pearce is a single mum of an adult daughter. Faith worked in banking, human resources, and quality management. Faith loves animals which includes her eight fur babies. She blogs for *All Things Wellness* and is a contributing author in *The Four-Fold Formula*. She is an artist, painter, and loves to cook.

Filomena Tripp is a retired Independent Living Specialist working tirelessly with people with disabilities. Filomena received awards from, The Massachusetts Rehabilitation Commission and Southeast Center for Independent Living. She now speaks at various events sharing her inspirational story. Her mission is to encourage others to live to their full potential.

Fran Asaro is the founder of Thrive Anyway, a consulting firm for entrepreneurs. Also, as the creator of The Senior Tuber Community, she helps mature women launch YouTube Channels to find their sense of purpose, leave a legacy, and earn extra money, all while having fun and supporting like-minded women. https://www.thriveanyway.com/

Frank Zaccari is a Business Adviser, TV Show Host and Speaker who served as a medic in the U.S.A.F. before spending over 20 years in high-tech. Frank is a 4X best-selling author. He's published eight books based on life-altering events. His Business & Personal Secrets series has three bestselling books in 12 months.

Gail Vilcu finds great joy in helping people LIVE LIFE NOW. As a certified relationship coach, she works with those ready to transform their past by removing personal barriers running their relationships since childhood. Her online coaching business, GVGreaterVision, was established in 2010 when her breakthrough became her life mission.

Gina Lobito is a Transformational Coach and Energy Intuitive with a background in bodywork and Vibrational Healing. Gina's approach to facilitating the healing journey is multidimensional, creating a bridge of MIND, BODY, and SPIRIT, grounding the experience through the instrumental body. Her passion to support clients' empowerment. www.soulinspiredreflections.com.

Gloria Sloan is CEO of Personal Dynamics, Inc., She is an author, professional certified life coach, and strategist. She has a passion for helping people to achieve their goals and find greater joy through self-discovery and using essential life skills. Her work focuses on transformation, ethical principles, empowerment, and personal development.

Known as The Heart Healer, Ilene Gottlieb has 50 plus years in Nursing and 28 plus years in Vibrational Healing creating holistic approaches to clearing energy blocks and promoting healing. She has served thousands of heart-centered clients globally as an International Speaker, Facilitator of Healing, Medical Intuitive and Ho'oponopono Educator. Website: IleneTheHeartHealer.com.

Jacki Long, B.A. psychology, is a Certified Jack Canfield Success Principles Trainer. Mentored by Sean Smith for over 10 years, Jacki is certified in Neurolinguistic Programming (NLP) and a featured trainer for advanced coaching certification courses. Jacki customizes programs for clients, helping them achieve their highest personal and professional goals.

Jacquel Tucker is an entrepreneur, non-profit founder, coach and published author who was born in a rural community in Jamaica. Through her signature My Purpose on Fire coaching program and online course she helps kingdom minded career professionals gain clarity, establish and launch their true purpose (business or non-profit) with influence and impact.

www.mypurposeonfire.com   connect@mypurposeonfire.com.

A native New Yorker, Jane McCarter-Caponigro is blessed to have had the opportunity to write a book, *YES I AM A to Z*; the words in the book are the start of gratitude in young minds giving them the power to develop self-esteem, self-worth, and confidence that every child deserves.

Janice Silva dreams big and brings others along. An entrepreneur and travel lover, Janice lives in Maui with her husband of 25 years. They wanted to live where the bougainvillea always blooms and have been blessed to do so. Janice offers Wellness Concierge services in Maui, Mexico, and Central California. JoyfulMauiWellness.com.

Janine Ouellette Sullivan is a writer. A forty-year career in social service taught her the value of compassion and action. Janine is the co-author of *Invisible Courage by Filomena Tripp* and *Paper Doll Kids by Deborah Beauvais.* Her latest work is a collection of original poetry titled *The Mushroom Tree*

Johnny Tan is a Keynote Speaker, Executive Career & Life Coach, Mentor, Multi-Award-Winning and bestselling author, and a talk show host. As a social entrepreneur, he is the Founder & CEO of From My Mama's Kitchen®, Publisher of "Inspirations for Better Living" digital magazine, and a REIKI Master Teacher & Healer.

Kathleen (Kat) O'Keefe-Kanavos is a three-time Breast Cancer Survivor seen on Dr. Oz, The DOCTORS, NBC, CBS. She's a Video Podcaster, Columnist, WEBE Books Publisher, and award-winning Author/Lecturer who promotes patient advocacy and connecting with Inner-guidance through Dreams for success in health, wealth, and relationships. Learn more @ KathleenOKeefeKanavos.com.

Kimberly Rinaldi, success coach, hypnotherapist, speaker, author, psychic-medium and radio show host, guides you through *Lessons in Joyful Living. Because the secret to life itself is JOY.* You'll connect with your intuition, self-healing, Divine intervention, miraculous outcomes and so much more. Join her for online events live from Southern California where she shares space with Mr. Rinaldi and their Basenji boy Jake. KimberlyRinaldi.com.

As an aging adult encountering digestive stress, energy loss, and finally unbearable pain, Kristi Tornabene had to do something to overcome all of this. Her family genes caused her grandma and her dad the inability to walk past the age of 70. She found that food makes a difference. https://www.keystobasichealth.com.

Laura Summa's career began in Commercial Art and advertising. She transitioned to illustrating. She is currently Vice President at Leadbelly Productions, a creative think tank producing products and services for children. Laura is married to Alan Jude Summa, also an artist. Together, they raised two grown children, and all reside in Northeast Pennsylvania.

Laura Frontiero, founder of BioRadiant Health, has served thousands of patients as a Nurse Practitioner for 22 years. As the 'energy lady,' Laura helps her clients renew mental focus, feel great in their bodies, and be productive again. When your body operates at your "Energy Edge," you are unstoppable, productive, happy, and fulfilled. LauraFrontiero.com

Leann Rhodes is a mom, previous elementary school teacher, certified Travel Agent, author, Sunday School teacher, and most of all, a child of God. Leann's life and testimony is one of resilience and hope. You can find both of her books on Amazon: *Rise Up Shine On,* and *Just Prevail*

Lisa Bianchino lives in Southeastern PA with Jesus and her two playful cats Mary and Clark. She loves going for walks, connecting with people, serving, traveling, reading God's Word, time with friends and family, and standing for God's truths. If you desire to share your story with me, reach out.

Bestselling author and speaker Lisa Caroglanian Dorazio's contributions appear globally in newspapers, magazines, and trade publications, and her co-authored book Conversations that Make a Difference: Stories Supporting a Bigger Vision. Embracing a servant mindset, Lisa founded CanAmeri Consulting, Inc. to always be a "Difference Maker" in the lives of others. www.canamericonsulting.com.

Lori Walker is a Usui Reiki Master, Holy Fire Reiki Master, and a blogger for *All Things Wellness*. She is a contributing author in *Mayhem to Miracles – Sacred Stories of Transformational Hope* and *The Four-Fold Formula for All Things Wellness*. She lives in Pittsburgh, Pennsylvania.

M. Yero Morris realized something was missing, he found himself immersed in a life's adventure of confronting his demons, having lost everything, and living off handouts. Through his warrior's spirit and the hero's journey, overcoming soul-crunching adversities, he found his authenticity, his happiness, joy, and humble, thankful self, and his way out of Hell.

Markus Wettstein. M.D. has practiced endocrinology for thirty years. He is a diabetes, metabolic and stress management specialist. He also works in energy medicine as a Licensed Bio-Well practitioner. He assists clients in improving their health and wellness by measuring their energy field, stress level, health status, and energy reserve via electro photonic imaging.

Maria Wynnyckyj currently works at a state college and is a writer/poet and is an amateur photographer. She is a proud mother of three grown children and two grandchildren and resides in the USA. Maria is inspired by art in all its forms because of what it reveals to her.

Marian and Jonathan Whitlock are the parents of 4 beautiful children ranging from 10-19 years of age. Originally from South Carolina, they now live in Leesburg, GA. Jonathan and Marian have been married for almost 22 years. They love volunteering in their community and coaching their children in sports.

Marina Garcia believes that behind everything is a blessing and that everyone we meet on our path is both a teacher and a gift. She believes it's easier to walk in gratitude and love than negativity. Marina says, "I am so happy for this opportunity to share my gratitude story. I hope it helps someone see those blessings are everywhere."

Marissa Bartley, a 17-year-old high school senior, will graduate in 2022 with her HS Diploma and Associate Degree in General Education from Germanna Community College. She'll go on to a four-year university as a nursing major while furthering her education in psychology. When Marissa isn't studying, she's working as a preschool teacher and waitress.

Mark Heidt is an award-winning writer/director/producer of $30 Million in half-hour infomercials. He has performed music at Carnegie Hall and fought forest fires in Idaho. Mark is husband to Sandy, father to Ken and Ruth, and grandfather to Graeme. His mission is to enlighten and empower. Faith is above all.

Mark Nelson O'Brien is the principal of O'Brien Communications Group (obriencg.com), a B2B brand-management and marketing firm he founded in 2004. He's also the co-founder and President of EinSource (einsource.com). And he's a lifelong writer. You can see all of his published work on Amazon.

Martiné Emmons is a Certified Life Coach, hosts a radio program, and enjoys helping entrepreneurs run their businesses as an Executive Virtual Assistant. Martiné loves staying active and finds travel, especially to ocean destinations, the best. She lives in Michigan with her husband and is a proud momma of three.

Melissa Zabower is a sister, aunt, writer, teacher, and friend. Above all, she believes in God, the Creator, Sustainer, and Provider. She lives in Emmaus, Pennsylvania. Melissa is writing two YA novels and a Bible study. Her book, *In the Shadow of Mr. Lincoln* is on Amazon.

Michelle Rene' Hammer, MS, LCPC, a Certified Pastoral Counselor, BREAKTHROUGH Coach, motivational speaker, bestselling author, and host of *Breakthrough Today with Michelle Rene'* helps women leaders navigate life's challenges in clinical and biblical ways. Her mission is to empower successful yet overextended Christian women to break through barriers to satisfying relationships and abundant joy-filled lives.

211

Mike Starr, adventurer, served on nuclear submarines, became an improvement team expert, and coached 100s with "Executive Coaching Services." Mike canoed from Pittsburgh to New Orleans in 54 days and hitchhiked for four months through the US, Mexico, and Guatemala on $3 daily. In retirement, Mike summited Mt. Kilimanjaro. His book, "Journey Into Peace," will be published in 2023.

Monica Talbot-Kerkes is an ESL teacher and the Program Director at Rowanwood Llama Farm in Sandy Hook, CT. She is also the Co-President and Co-Author of the award-winning children's book series "The Llove Llama & Friends." She resides in CT with her husband and two children.

Noel Vandegrift resides in Pennsylvania with the love of her life JT, their two children, Aiden and Kinsleigh, and their three cats. Noel works full-time in the medical field. She enjoys spending time with her family, redoing furniture, and, more importantly, spending time with the Lord.

Nova Jane E. Alcoran started her artistic journey with freelance coloring projects and teaming up with Aljon Inertia. She fell in love with the creative process and discovered her purpose in working with Aljon to create beautiful children's books. Nova lives in the Philippines, and her work with Aljon is seen worldwide.

P.J. is an international resiliency speaker, trainer, coach, consultant, author, former wheelchair athlete, meditation teacher, traveler, and artist. He founded two non-profits and four disabled sports programs. Although his disability was expected to take his life by age seven, his desire to live an exciting and purposeful life prevailed. Learn more at PJsWisdom.com

Patricia Froehlich, retired State's Attorney for Connecticut's Judicial of Windham, is currently a yoga teacher in Florida. She is grateful for support from friends and family but most grateful for her husband's encouragement. From running a 5K to applying to be state's attorney, she believed she could, and she did!

Peggy Willms has 30+ years as a fitness trainer, sports nutritionist, personal and exec health, wellness, and life coach. She is an entrepreneur, and co-author of the book, *The Four-Fold Formula* with many children's' books in the works. She hosts The Coach Peggy Show and hosts wellness retreats. She is a featured contributor for BizCatalyst360. She is a mother of two adult sons (one contributing to this book) and a cool grandma.

Dr. Rachelle Simpson Sweet is a Certified Epigenetic Wellness Coach and Ph.D. in Neuropsychology. Through biological individuality and understanding genetics, she helps women design a plan to go from being fatigued, stressed, and not sleeping to having more energy and clarity, so they can wake up with confidence and rock their day.

Rene Kamstra, an internationally recognized businesswoman and communications expert has 35+ years of experience in consulting and coaching leading corporate executives and entrepreneurs from humble beginnings to $millions. Rene teaches people how to communicate excellently, sell without pressure, become unstuck, and grow businesses. Tony Robbins, Chet Holmes, Sally Hogshead, Corelogic, VISA, and Wells Fargo are among her many clients. ReneKamstra.com.

Robin Walton has a Master's in Education and grew up in Philadelphia. She has been married for 31 years to Rich Walton. They have two sons. She is a student at Mission Seminary. She has birthed a ministry, Redeeming Us Through Healing, to serve women who have suffered serious scars in their past.

Sally Sarah Adukwu-Bolujoko is an author, speaker, management, and leadership consultant. She served as an adviser to President Ebele Goodluck Jonathan of the Federal Republic of Nigeria, who conferred the prestigious honor of Officer of the Order of the Niger, OON. Sally's latest book, *Leading Without Title,* is on Amazon.com.

Samantha Larkin lives in the suburbs of Philly with her five cats. After about 14 years in IT, God brought her back to ministering through portrait experiences. She loves praying, spending time with friends, watching Christian movies, going to the beach and now taking care of the temple He gave her by making healthy choices.

Sandra (Sandy) Heidt is a retired teacher and coach of St. Petersburg High School, Florida's champion swim and track teams. She is an avid scrapbooker, mother to daughter Ruth, son Kenneth, and grandmother to Graeme. Sandy and her college sweetheart husband, Mark, have been married for 47 years.

P. A. Serena Hemmer, MSW, LCSW holds a Master's in Clinical Social Work. Serena is an ordained Metaphysical Minister and Cosmic Sound Shaman. She has written and illustrated *Pearl's Wisdom Books* and *Galactic Light Language, An Experiencer's Experience.* Serena's mission is to assist others to remember their miraculous magnificence.

Shannon Barker is a Florida native with a passion for health and fitness leading her to become a registered dietitian and earn a Master's in Exercise Science. Shannon specializes in helping women reach their goals through behavior modification coaching by identifying their root cause of health discrepancies.

Sharla Charpentier is a mother of four, lawyer, writer, and artist. She co-authored *The Llove Llama Travels the 7 Continents, Ned the Narwhal Voyages the 5 Oceans,* and *Bob the Sloth Explores South America* in The *Llove Llama and Friends Series.* She also contributed her story to *Mayhem to Miracles.* TheLloveLlamaAndFriends.com

Sharlene R Prince, the Royalty Mindset Elevation Coach, mother. entrepreneur, author, and mentor has a Masters in Human Resource Development and Administration. Sharlene focuses on empowering women and children with skills to overcome their circumstances. The Royalty Mindset Elevation enables them to be self-reliant and develop a mindset of Rising Above.

Dr. Sharon Martin holds a doctorate in Physiology and graduated from Johns Hopkins School of Medicine in Internal Medicine. She is a certified graduate of the Healing the Light Body curriculum of the Four Winds Society, a premier training program in shamanic energy medicine. She also is the host of two radio shows, Maximum Medicine and Sacred Magic, aired on Transformation Talk Radio.

Sophia Long is a scholar studying sociology and women, gender, and sexuality studies at IUPUI. She is an avid activist and intersectional feminist, currently living in the Midwest with her partner and two cats. sophialongwrites@gmail.com

Susan Sheppard is a speaker, writer, trainer, and coach who is passionate about true intimacy and her crusade against indifferent relationships. She is the author of the book *How to Get What You Want From Your Man Anytime.* Susan also published her daughter, Stephanie's children's book, *Is There a Bunny at Your House.* Susansheppard.com.

Author, speaker, humanitarian, and coach, Sylvia Morrison stepped away from her 30+ year-teaching career to follow her heart's Calling. Founder of Links Across Borders, a non-profit organization that co-creates libraries and facilitates educational programs for children in Ghana. Her bestselling book; *Inspired Living: A Guide to Ignite Joy and Prosperity*, shares her personal journey creating the life she desires. https://sylviamorrison.com/

Sylvie Plant is a passionate, caring, bold, full of energy and vitality woman entrepreneur who uses her voice to make a difference in people's lives. Through my coaching, mentoring, and facilitating, I empower people to reinvent themselves and achieve their goals while creating time and financial freedom.

Tammy Hader is an essay contributor to Medium.com, BizCatalyst360 and WebMD. She enjoys caring for her mom, cooking for her husband, and serving her two cats with the royal attention they deserve. Tammy is working on publishing her memoir titled Walking Old Roads for release in 2023.

Tanner Willms is a logistics specialist and six years in the oil and gas industry as an NDT inspector. After a tragic motocross accident spiraled into an alcohol addiction, he focused on sobriety and raising a family. He and his wife, Brittney, welcomed their first son, Crew, in April 2021 and are expecting their second in the spring of 2023. As a recovered alcoholic he hopes his story will inspire others to keep fighting.

Tasha Chen is known for her success with entrepreneurs. Her easy and relaxed approach to getting things done and her intuitive downloads and energy have produced off-the-chart results. A coach, speaker, and thought leader, Tasha can keep you aligned and focused on your goals while giving you the attraction principles and leadership strategies to shift from overwhelmed to overjoyed. TashaChen.com

Tyra Glaze is a single mother of two young kings. At 29, Tyra was diagnosed with breast cancer. She was devastated but VERY determined to FIGHT! Tyra has truly exemplified her strength as a "Warrior" and a "Hero" to her sons, family, friends, and others. Find her children's book, My *Mom is My Hero,* on Amazon.

Since being the victim of a near-death hit-and-run accident while on foot, Vincent A. Lanci has used his journey and experiences to normalize the conversation around mental health and inspire entrepreneurship. He is shattering mental health stigma as an International Selling Author, Speaker, and Podcaster.

Native New Yorker, Will Pollock, is an award-winning author, blogger, photographer, multimedia journalist, and creator of CrankyYank.com. Now in Midtown Atlanta, Will is a permaculture and green-living evangelist and lifelong tennis player. As the world's proudest papa to Cam, his new children's book, *Gentle with Gertie*, is a story of human-and-furry siblings, available on Amazon.

About the Author

Teresa Velardi is an author, publisher, host of the *Conversations That Make a Difference* podcast, coach, and potter.

Michelangelo, the famous 15th-century artist and sculptor said, "*Every block of stone has a statue inside it, and it is the sculptor's task to discover it.*" His job was to remove the excess stone to reveal the beauty within.

Similarly, Teresa uses the art of pottery to illustrate that each ball of clay can and will be transformed into a beautiful work of art with the touch of the potter's hand. Teresa guides her clients through the process of centering, molding, shaping, and walking through the fire of challenges to effect positive life change as they gracefully and powerfully embrace the work of art they already are.

Teresa found her passion and purpose through life's challenges while trusting God's plan. Faith in God, gratitude, and giving are her heart. Her abilities as a writer, editor, and publisher are vital ingredients she brings to those who share their message with the world on her podcast or through her publishing platform.

Her daily quiet time, writing, and gratitude practice keep Teresa focused on her God-given purpose as life unfolds in this ever-changing world. We all have a story to tell and a heartfelt message to share. What's your message?

DailyGiftBookSeries.com
AuthenticEndeavorsPublishing.com
ConversationsThatMakeADifference.com

Gratitude Story Take-Aways

Name of Story:

Author:

How I connected to the Story:

Gratitude Story Take-Aways

Name of Story:

Author:

How I connected to the Story:

Gratitude Story Take-Aways

Name of Story:

Author:

How I connected to the Story:

Gratitude Story Take-Aways

Name of Story:

Author:

How I connected to the Story:

Gratitude Story Take-Aways

Name of Story:

Author:

How I connected to the Story

Gratitude Story Take-Aways

Name of Story:

Author:

How I connected to the Story

Gratitude Story Take-Aways

Name of Story:

Author:

How I connected to the Story

The Daily Gift Book Series Continues:

Coming Soon

A Daily Gift of Kindness
and
A Daily Gift of Hope

Do you have a story for one of the
next books in the series?

Learn how you can
be a contributing author at:

DailyGiftBookSeries.com

Made in United States
North Haven, CT
22 December 2022

30030539R00134